Advance Praise

I congratulate Dr Sujata Bhat for her vision in writing this outstanding, easy-to-read Pocket Planner for Pregnancy. It is a boon to all prospective parents. This attractively laid-out book equips women with the essential knowledge to experience a safe pregnancy. It educates fathers about the equally important care before, during and after pregnancy. Together, a must-have guide for couples.

—Professor Pratap Kumar
Department of Obstetrics & Gynecology,
Kasturba Medical College, Manipal (Karnataka)

Dr Sujata Bhat's planner is a treasure-trove of valuable knowledge on pregnancy. It is a ready-reckoner that will enable every parent to navigate this joyful and complex phase with confidence and ease. Her vast skills and experience as a seasoned Obstetrician and Gynecologist accompany this planner.

—Vanita Nayak Mukherjee
Activist, Researcher, Former Program Officer, Ford Foundation

Dr Sujata Bhat's Pocket Planner for Pregnancy is an absolute must for all those planning a family. This lucidly written book encompasses the most pertinent topics from pre-pregnancy counselling, diet and exercise, dos and don'ts to providing valuable home remedy tips to deal with common problems during pregnancy, delivery, post delivery and the currently advised vaccinations for the newborn.

—Prof Krishnendu Gupta
Professor and Unit Head,
Dept of Obstetrics & Gynaecology,
Vivekananda Institute of Medical Sciences,
WBUHS, Kolkata
Adjunct Professor,
Dept of Obstetrics & Gynaecology,
Kasturba Medical College, MAHE, Manipal

Your Pocket Planner *for* Pregnancy

DR SUJATA BHAT

Vitasta

We dedicate this book to our Mother,
Smt Kanaka Durgamba and Father,
Ex Captain Bulusu Jagdishwar Gandhi to
whom we owe our lives.

Sujata (Author) and Jyothsna (Editor)

Published by
Renu Kaul Verma
Vitasta Publishing Pvt Ltd
2/15, Ansari Road, Daryaganj,
New Delhi - 110 002
info@vitastapublishing.com

ISBN: 978-93-86473-84-4

First Edition 2020
MRP ₹ 399

Illustrations by Surajit Santra
Photos by Harshit Walia
Typeset & Cover Design by Somesh Kumar Mishra
Printed by Vikas Computer and Printers

Contents

Acknowledgements

MY SINCERE GRATITUDE to Ms Renu Kaul Verma and her staff from Vitasta Publishing Private Limited, who have been instrumental in taking this book from manuscript to print and making it accessible to all those readers in search of practical pointers to planning for a baby. Thanks to Ms Veena Batra and Mr Somesh Kumar Mishra for their helpful tips and expert implementation. When I expressed to Ms Renu that I wanted the book to "belong in a handbag and not on a shelf", her reaction indicated that she heard me. I sensed that we were in sync as her suggestions were spot on and it has been a delightful experience working with her. One person who walked with me once the idea of writing the book took root was Smita Jain, for whose unconditional support I owe a big thank you. Thanks also to my colleagues, Dr Anita Kaul, Dr Akshatha Sharma and Dr Lavanya Rai for their thoughtful, professional viewpoints that greatly enhanced the quality of the book. My special thanks to Ms Swati Gosain for her constructive comments on the text and illustrations.

My heartfelt credit to my family—daughter, Aakanksha, who insisted on being the first to read the early draft and helped me sort the images; husband, Anil; and brother-in-law, Ashoka, who occasionally made casual remarks about the script which usually turned out to be astute and noteworthy. Most important of all credit goes to my sister, Jyothsna, who played a pivotal role as the editor in the making of this book. Her detailed, critical comments and perspectives from a non-medical point of view while keeping the Indian reader in mind, shaped the book. Publishing this book is a loving tribute to our parents. My deepest gratitude to my late mother, Smt Bulusu Kanaka Durgamba and my late father, Captain Bulusu Jagdishwar Gandhi, due to whose hopes and constant support I am able to help other families today.

—Dr Sujata Bhat

Introduction

TODAY, WE LIVE in complex environments, particularly in urban areas, where small families, multiple daily tasks and long commutes are commonplace. Does this sound familiar to you? As a couple considering parenthood, you are sometimes left feeling that reliable advice is not easy to come by, as one is pressed for time to do one's own research, trusted sources such as older members of immediate family live far away, or simply that questions about pregnancy are too delicate to ask. At other times, some self-reliant couples may prefer to plan parenthood independently even when their families are easily accessible. Others may seek better information after a difficult prior experience. For all these reasons, a handy book with sufficient information to induce confidence may be just the friend you are in search of.

And then there are reasons from my perspective as an obstetrician and gynaecologist. Over several decades of my practice, I have answered many anxious questions and observed unfortunate situations that repeat themselves in one form or another. Even today, when reproductive medical theory and practice has advanced in so many ways, young couples report for their first consultation only after the third month of pregnancy, often as advised by elders at home. By this time it is too late to access much of the valuable information, so vital to shed light on the health of both the baby and pregnancy. Then there are working women who reluctantly give up their jobs believing that bed rest is necessary, now that they are pregnant. Similarly, some couples, fearful of the consequences, skip ultrasound procedures only to regret their folly when a problem is detected later, often too late to treat. As you can understand, the examples described above are all very distressing to a caring doctor who knows that all the stress and tension may not have been necessary "if only they knew". I believe that educating consumers enough to give them a chance to avoid such mistakes is a worthwhile contribution to society and to the patients I serve. After all, pregnancy should be a happy, positive experience.

The approach in this book is to touch upon the key areas of planning and preparing to bring a baby home. The information in the chapters that follow is arranged so that even in the case of an unplanned pregnancy, the couple in question can get on track and do what is needed for the best possible outcome.

In India, daily routines and food have evolved based on age old practices rooted in indigenous medical traditions, the environmental climate we live in, and socio-economic systems we depend on and in which we thrive. Although the information presented here is based on the current state of knowledge and clinical practice which is based on prescribed guidelines in allopathic medicine it is set in the context of the lifestyle and family dynamics of the Indian consumer. In this way it provides practical suggestions from up-to-date medical practice against a background that respects everyday life as we know it, involving resources that are normally accessible to us.

The book is intended as a brief primer, yet it is comprehensive enough to cover the key topics. It is deliberately concise with informative tables and images to be user-friendly. It is divided into thirteen chapters that may be read together or individually referenced when needed. Popularly recognised non-English names and terms used by Indians are incorporated wherever appropriate for added clarity. Medical terms appear in the narrative to familiarise readers with them and to increase patients' general awareness of common pregnancy related concerns. These terms are defined in the glossary provided at the end of each chapter and sometimes in the text itself. They are marked by superscripts. The reader is urged to read the description of the entry in the glossary before returning to the sentence in which it appears. Having read the words beforehand many patients are able to get more out of their visit to the doctor by asking detailed questions and leave feeling confident about understanding and absorbing the advice given.

The unmistakable message of the book is to inform all those unsure of where to begin that there is help that you can seek; consult medical guidance from a doctor who is qualified to take you through all the steps to a good outcome.

Chapter 1 entitled "Pre-pregnancy Counselling" is for those contemplating pregnancy, the primary objective being to create awareness regarding the importance of visiting a doctor even before planning to have a baby. The chapter touches upon the need for testing to ascertain if both you and your partner are healthy enough to proceed with planning for a comfortable pregnancy and healthy baby. The information here also suggests that it is possible to be adequately ready to face problems that may be foreseen.

Chapter 2 is an extension of chapter 1 in some ways, describing tests and visits to your doctor. The distinction, however, is that while the former dwells on why a visit to the doctor is critical even before you are pregnant, the second chapter focuses on what to expect in each visit to your doctor once you are already pregnant. The information in chapter 2 helps you to prepare for your appointments, perhaps also to set aside enough "leave" if you are working or to budget your finances. You may want to gather any information or documents showing results of prior diagnoses to share with your doctor after reading the material covered here.

By chapter 3 you move past planning. For eight weeks past conception your womb carries what is known as the embryo. Beyond this period it is called a foetus—your baby has progressed to the foetal stage whose life, in spite of much research, is still an enigma. What we do know is that by now the foetus has developed the senses of touch, taste, smell, hearing and sight and has established a connection to your emotions and behaviour.

Every pregnant woman is eager to know what to eat, as she instinctively wants to do everything she can to nurture a healthy baby while also making the task as easy and pleasant as possible. Chapter 4 tries to answer that question by describing what a healthy diet should consist of and also which foods are to be consumed in moderation or avoided altogether. This chapter describes a "pregnancy spread" with snacks and meals relevant to the way an Indian consumes food to stay nourished.

You will notice physiological changes as your pregnancy progresses, some good and others not so good. Nevertheless, you want to continue to keep the sparkle in your looks and feel confident about yourself. You want to be well groomed as a means to remain cheerful when confronted by new situations.

Chapter 5 suggests a few tips on how to be that self-assured, beautiful, pregnant woman.

Whether working outside or inside the home, some additional thought about your own safety and that of the foetus should be part of your planning.

Chapter 6 proposes arrangements to increase your physical comfort to get through your day. It also encourages you to pay attention to where and how you work to protect yourself and your foetus from any harmful effects of the surroundings or other aspects of your job.

Chapter 7 says that being active and energetic while remaining mindful of your state is healthy for normal pregnancies, as determined by your doctor. Here you can read about how exercise can help you, exercise options, your limitations and the precautions you must take to gain the benefits without harming yourself.

Next, chapter 8 suggests some quick fixes and home remedies that can tackle familiar annoyances and ailments that accompany pregnancy while also stressing that one should be sensible and consult the doctor when symptoms are unusual or continue to persist.

Chapter 9 presents scenarios in which you can find practical distractions through the long months of your pregnancy. Shopping for yourself and gathering essentials to care for the newborn are fulfilling. As the major part of the pregnancy is behind, ceremonies are organised to celebrate motherhood and shower blessings on the baby-to-come. In some instances, celebrations can be quite trendy.

Chapter 10 addresses the understanding that both parents have to show in carrying out their respective roles and responsibilities. In particular, the couple is urged to pay special attention to preparing the future sibling or siblings, if any, to welcome their new brother or sister to the family with a positive attitude. A few reminders to help you get ready to bring the newborn home from the hospital are also mentioned.

If there is one phase where a knowledgeable adult is sorely missed, it is probably when the excited, newly-expanded family arrives home. There is no doctor or nurse to hold your hand and how well you cope depends on all the arrangements you made while planning ahead. The purpose of the last three chapters is to help you do just that. "The Awakening" or chapter 11 addresses the mother's recovery during the all-important confinement period after delivery.

Chapter 12 provides some answers to all those basic questions that arise seemingly at every turn relating to newborn care, suggesting also that this is Dad's chance to bond with his baby. As it is easy to forget in the thick of all the unceasing activity, chapter 13 sets out by reviewing precautionary vaccinations, maintaining your health and air travel with an infant under the changed circumstances. The book then concludes with the whole journey coming full circle in this final chapter as the parents bring their life as a couple back to normalcy once more. Normalcy, however, implies that you can get pregnant all over again immediately after the six-week recovery period. For this reason, you are informed about the options for contraception at your disposal. Simultaneously, you are urged to consider the wisdom of spacing pregnancies and to use the birth control methods most suitable to you to help manage it. Of course, when you decide the time has come to add another member to the family, you are reminded of the all-important trip to the doctor for—you guessed it—pre-pregnancy counselling!

OCTOBER

CHAPTER 1

Pre-Pregnancy Counselling

IF YOU ARE a couple getting ready for a baby, then your first step should be to seek *pre-pregnancy counselling* from your doctor. Through pre-pregnancy counselling you will receive guidance on all aspects of planning and preparing to ensure a smooth pregnancy and a healthy baby. Ideally, the counselling session should be attended by the couple as the health and lifestyle of each of the parents has consequences and influences the outcome. Furthermore, it is prudent to visit the doctor for counselling even if it is not your first pregnancy. Couples who have had a poor pregnancy outcome from a previous attempt will benefit considerably from careful preparation the next time around.

The total duration of pregnancy is considered to be 40 weeks. During this time, the most crucial phase in foetal[1] development takes place as early as in the first trimester of pregnancy (there are three trimesters: first, second and third; each trimester consists of three months). For this reason, it is highly recommended that prospective parents receive pre-pregnancy counselling well before this critical period. This allows pre-emptive steps to be taken to address avoidable problems in good time.

Primarily, your own health and nutritional intake can affect your baby's growth and development. Some key elements in this context are—Body Mass Index or BMI[2], balance of vitamins and minerals in the body, and lifestyle. Proactive pre-pregnancy counselling will suggest ways in which you can prepare your body for a trouble-free pregnancy under normal circumstances, or to address any risk factors you may encounter.

According to Indian standards, a BMI of 18.5 to 22.9 is considered normal. A BMI that is less than 18.5, as in an underweight woman, can lead to a baby with low birth weight. A woman whose BMI falls between 23 and 24.9 is considered overweight on the other hand (see Table 1.1), and faces the risk of developing Preeclampsia[3] and Gestational Diabetes[4].

Table 1.1 Nutritional status based on the World Health Organization (WHO) and "Asian criteria" values

Nutritional Status	WHO criteria BMI cut-off	"Asian criteria" BMI cut-off
Underweight	<18.5	<18.5
Normal	18.5–24.9	18.5–22.9
Overweight	25–29.9	23–24.9
Pre-obese	-	25–29.9
Obese		
Obese Type 1 (obese)	30–40	30–40
Obese Type 2 (morbid obese)	40.1–50	40.1–50
Obese Type 3 (super obese)	>50	>50

Source: *Body Mass Index Calculator for Men and Women–Indian BMI Chart posted by Mehnaz Farooque, last updated February 1, 2019. Medically reviewed by R Sindhu Vas, Masters in Food Science and Nutrition; www.truweight.in*

Body mass index (BMI)

A measure called Body Mass Index or BMI is used to classify individuals into different weight categories taking their height and weight into account. It is calculated as the person's weight in kilograms divided by his or her height in meters squared. The result is used to describe one as being underweight, normal, overweight or obese. Although the measure has its limitations it is considered handy to easily identify those who are most likely to be at risk for weight-related concerns, chief among them being diabetes (type 2), heart disease and hypertension.

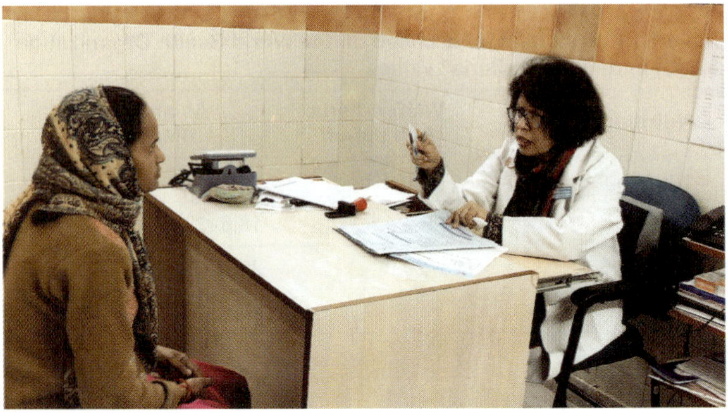

Preconception care to improve pregnancy outcomes is relevant for all women of reproductive age group (WHO).

The ranges in Table 1.1 show the international criteria and those relevant for Indian adults. Recognising that the risk of facing weight-related diseases is higher in Asians relative to non-Asian populations at lower BMI measures, the WHO corrected the cut-off points downward to categorise overweight Asians. So, an Indian is overweight if the BMI is between 22.9 and 24.9 relative to the international range between 24.9 and 29.9. Correspondingly, what this implies is that Indians are at risk of weight-related diseases starting even at BMIs as low as 22.9. Indians with BMIs ranging from 25 to 29.9 are considered pre-obese. Incidentally, while there is a view that BMI ranges should ideally be different between men and women too, due to dissimilarity in body structures and fat distribution, the existing ranges are applied without any correction.

Inadequate presence of vitamin B9 or folic acid in the body can lead to defects of the brain and spinal cord. However, evidence suggests that if a small dose of folic acid is taken daily, neural tube defects[5] can be prevented to a considerable extent. A low daily dose of 0.5 milligram is considered sufficient, unless you are at risk for neural tube defects. In the latter circumstance, a higher dose of 5 milligrams daily may be required. If you are planning a pregnancy and decide to consult a doctor first, you will probably be advised to start taking folic acid at least three months in advance. Similarly, vitamin D3 is required for proper absorption of calcium. The musculoskeletal system in the baby forms and grows sourcing calcium from the mother. Vitamin D3 is vital both for the overall health of the developing baby and to help replenish used up calcium in the mother. For this reason, the doctor may check if you have sufficient vitamin D3 and prescribe it if necessary. Another necessary mineral is iron, a key ingredient in red blood cells that transport oxygen from the lungs to various tissues in the body. So expect to be tested for iron-deficiency anaemia because you want to prepare to be energetic and ensure unrestricted growth in the baby.

Prenatal counselling aims to assess and optimize the woman's health, educate, and help her through her pregnancy. Timely diagnosis of high blood sugar levels, which can cause malformations[6], can help you address the problem. Likewise, your doctor will suggest ways to overcome deficiency, if any, of iodine in your body. The intention here is to prevent Hypothyroidism[7], which can adversely affect the baby's Intelligence Quotient[8] (IQ). Iodine Deficiency Disorder (IDD) is the leading cause of avoidable mental retardation. In spite of running a successful campaign to educate the public about the importance of iodine in the diet (see reference for NIDDCP), many Indians, particularly in rural households are still unaware of the critical role of iodised salt.

> Seek counselling before conception for detection of health ailments and timely interventions.

Couples often ask their doctors about when to time a pregnancy. Advancing the age to start a family appears to be a trend in modern lifestyles, particularly those of partners who are both in busy careers. From a medical perspective, such an approach or decision is undesirable for a variety of reasons. The probability of conceiving diminishes as you grow older because the production of a number of good quality eggs and sperm decreases with time. Also, once pregnant, the likelihood of the onset of diabetes or high blood pressure, and premature deliveries is higher in older women.

A large percentage of pregnancies are unplanned. Although the advantages of early pre-pregnancy testing are missed in such circumstances, it is wise for the couple to be counselled by a doctor as soon as possible. Pregnancy counselling is still relevant because you and your partner will receive guidance in the steps to be taken going forward and preparing the mother to successfully carry and deliver the baby.

Of particular value, as a result of pre-pregnancy counselling, is the detection of genetic disorders that couples may be completely unaware of. However, they are of utmost relevance to the pregnancy outcome. While a simple blood test can detect only a subset of the many possible disorders, it is still worthwhile using one to identify even the few, such as, Thalassemia[9] and Sickle Cell Disorders[10]. Another objective of getting blood tests done at this stage is to rule out the presence of infections, such as Hepatitis[11] and Sexually Transmitted Diseases[12].

Moreover, women with compromised mental health, or who suffer from medical disorders such as diabetes, high blood pressure, thyroid conditions, epilepsy, heart disease or tuberculosis need pre-pregnancy counselling as they will have to pay special attention to associated difficulties. Have a frank and honest discussion with your doctor about health issues and diagnoses you are already aware of. Talk about those pertaining not only to your own history but also the mental, medical and genetic histories of family members. If possible, bring any relevant documents or even the afflicted family member to help the doctor make an informed assessment. Tell your doctor about all the medications you are taking, as in some instances the dosages may need to be modified or the medications may have to be changed altogether to prevent complications from occurring. Unless these complications, if known to be present, are dealt with in advance and the guidance given is followed, they can cause structural malformations or miscarriages, or even premature labour pains.

There are some known genetic disorders prevalent in India, such as Thalassaemia (more widespread in West Bengal, Maharashtra, Gujarat and Punjab), and Glucose-6-phosphate dehydrogenase or G6PD deficiency[13] (observed more in southern India). Congenital hypothyroidism[14] and some kinds of muscular atrophy[15] are also among them. For this reason, while discussing your medical history with the doctor, be sure to share the medical histories of family members also. It is important to mention any consanguineous marriage[16] or the existence of any familial genetic disease. If there are chances of a family member being a carrier[17] of a genetic disorder, you can be screened for factors indicating a risk to you, and if positive, diagnostic tests can be done to rule out the presence of the disease.

During initial discussion with your doctor, you will learn about a number of vaccines that are essential to prevent infections. For example, German measles or Rubella[18] is an infection that can be very dangerous, especially if contracted in the first three months of pregnancy. The doctor will talk to you about vaccinating yourself against Rubella and Varicella or chickenpox before you get pregnant. It is necessary to wait for at least four weeks after taking the vaccinations before planning a pregnancy. Discussion on immunization will also include the Hepatitis B vaccine and the Influenza vaccine.

Your lifestyle is of special concern in the context of pregnancy. For example, you may indulge in gardening but now you will have to be mindful about wearing gloves when handling components like soil, compost, plants and tools to minimise exposure to infections and injuries. Or you may have cats as pets and will need to use gloves to dispose excreta, followed by washing hands thoroughly to protect yourself from contracting an infection like Toxoplasmosis[19]. If you

> A comfortable pregnancy and healthy baby depend on the health of both Dad and Mom.

smoke, consume alcohol or drugs, then be prepared to be advised to modify your lifestyle. Similarly, precautionary measures will be suggested if you are a coffee and/or tea drinker too.

Work towards an ideal body weight, as advised by your doctor. Eat a balanced diet and exercise on a regular basis (more on this in chapters 4 and 7). Most importantly, undergo all the necessary tests that your doctor advises during pre-pregnancy counselling, before taking the plunge into the nine-month roller coaster ride!

Glossary

1. **Foetal:** Conception is the process of becoming pregnant. It is the time when the sperm meets the egg that has been released from the ovary. The word 'foetal' pertains to 'foetus' which is a developing human from eight weeks after conception until birth.

2. **BMI:** A measure that tells you the ratio of fat to muscle in your body. Body Mass Index is calculated as weight in kilograms / $(\text{height in metres})^2$.

3. **Preeclampsia:** Refers to increase in blood pressure after 20 weeks of pregnancy.

4. **Gestational diabetes:** Diabetes contracted during pregnancy which usually reverts to a normal state after delivery.

5. **Neural tube defects:** Birth defects of the brain and spinal cord and their coverings.

6. **Malformations:** Abnormalities of body structures.

7. **Hypothyroidism:** The thyroid gland is a butterfly-shaped structure in the front of the neck. The gland uses iodine to produce some vital hormones. If an adequate quantity of thyroid hormone is not produced, then the condition is called Hypothyroidism.

8. **Intelligence Quotient or IQ:** A measure of intelligence represented as a score calculated from different intelligence tests.

9. **Thalassemia:** An inherited blood disorder in which the body makes an abnormal type of haemoglobin.

10. **Sickle cell disorders:** A group of inherited red blood cell defects.

11. **Hepatitis:** Infection of the liver.

12. **Sexually transmitted diseases:** Infections transmitted through sexual contact.

13. **G6PD deficiency:** A condition in which some medications, stresses and infections cause red blood cells to break down due to the lack of G6PD (an enzyme).

14. **Congenital hypothyroidism:** Iodine is necessary for the thyroid gland to produce hormones. Not enough iodine in the mother and infant is one of the known causes of insufficient production of thyroid hormone in infants, a condition called congenital hypothyroidism. Congenital hypothyroidism may also arise due to genetic and other factors.

15. **Muscular atrophy:** Spinal muscular atrophy is a genetic disorder that makes muscles weaker over time, affecting movement.

16. **Consanguineous marriage:** Marriage between second cousins or closer relatives.

17. **Carrier:** A person who has inherited a form of a gene that does not display the symptoms of a genetic trait but carries it nevertheless.

18. **Rubella:** Also known as German measles, it is a contagious viral infection recognised by a distinctive red rash. It can be prevented by a specifically administered vaccine.

19. **Toxoplasmosis:** A parasitic infection (one due to an organism living in the body as a parasite) that can threaten the health of an unborn child.

Phew! I Am pregnant

CHAPTER 2

Congratulations! You are Pregnant

Begin with doctor-guided antenatal care

THE ALL-IMPORTANT, "antenatal" phase refers to the time that elapses between the last menstrual period before you became pregnant and the date of delivery. For normal pregnancies, this phase usually consists of 40 weeks. In everyday parlance, the term "pregnancy" is generally perceived as everything that happens during this period. This is a crucial time when your baby forms and grows. It is during this period that you can address any avertable problems and ensure that the experience is as stress free as possible. Consequently, the primary objectives of antenatal care are to ensure that you are as normal and prepared as you can be to deliver a healthy baby and both you and your baby emerge from this period free from health-related complications.

> Ultrasonography involves sound waves and no electromagnetic radiation so it is considered safe for the baby.

Unfortunately, there is a myth that ultrasonography[1] is harmful to the foetus and that early blood tests are best avoided. Based on this false belief, pregnant women are often discouraged from consulting a doctor before completing three months of pregnancy. Below, you will see why current medical practice advises otherwise and what you can expect from doctor-guided antenatal care.

Early test for the best

Ideally, for healthy pregnant women, the first appointment needs to be prior to 13 weeks into pregnancy because the first trimester offers a large volume of valuable information about your readiness. In fact, two appointments may be necessary in early pregnancy. The first trimester is a critical time when certain detected problems can be tackled and nipped in the bud.

Your first visit may include a number of blood tests, some of which are repeated every three months. Please do not hesitate to have them done because each test has a specific significance. Some tests may involve your partner as well, so alert him about the need to set aside time for these visits. Medical afflictions that can be ruled out early through these tests are—Thalassemia[2] (a genetic blood disorder common in India), Thyroid[3] complications, Anaemia[4], Rubella[5] (also known as German measles) and Diabetes[6] (a disease of much current interest, that can be identified from a simple glucose test). Hepatitis B[7], Hepatitis C[7] and Sexually Transmitted Diseases[8] (STDs) are also screened for at this time. Tests also determine your blood group which provides necessary and useful information. It is important to undergo these tests because every condition, mentioned above, can adversely affect your baby's development and so its presence or

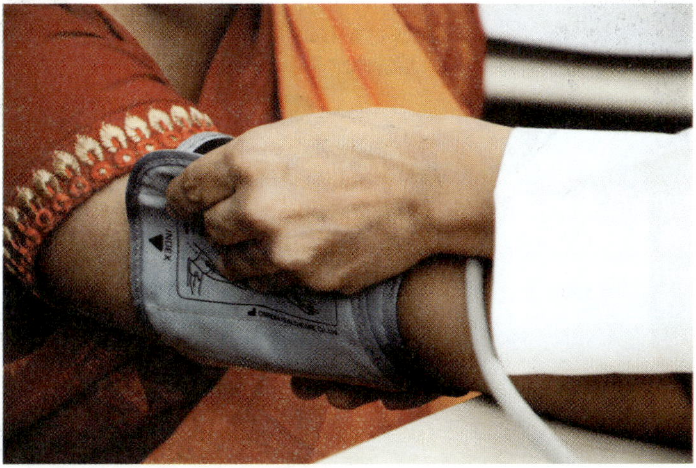

Measurement is done with the correct cuff size. Blood pressure is recorded with the arm resting on the table at the level of the heart.

absence must be determined early. For this reason, an early diagnosis is recommended.

Ultrasonography uses ultrasound technology which involves sound waves and not electromagnetic radiation[9], so it is radiation free. Further, medical ultrasound imaging for pregnancy is specifically designed to produce scans for medical diagnosis safely.

According to routine procedure, five ultrasound scans are required in all. Specifically, three are done in the first 20 weeks, the next scan at 28 weeks and the last scan at 36 weeks. Out of these, the first is a scan to date the pregnancy, detect the heartbeat and confirm that

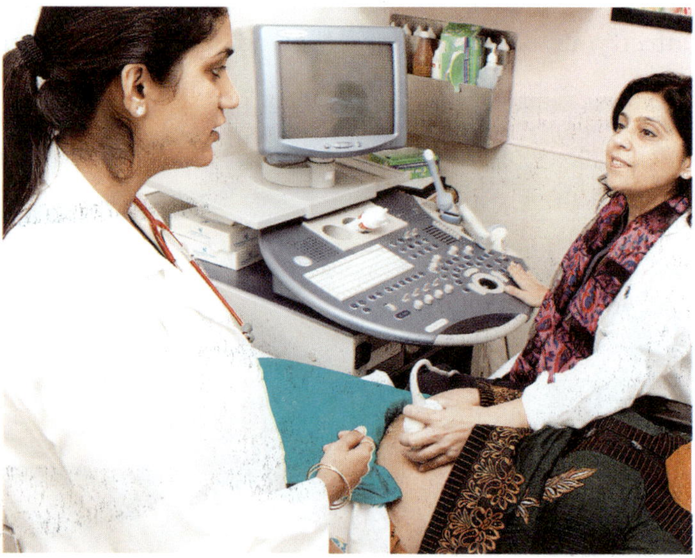

Ultrasound scanning in pregnancy helps in screening for abnormalities and also monitors the growth of the baby.

the pregnancy is inside the uterus and not outside it. The next two ultrasound scans between 11 and 13 weeks 6 days and between 18 and 20 weeks are particularly important for detecting foetal developmental abnormalities. The last two scans track the baby's growth. So, if you are unable to have all the five scans done due to financial or other reasons, then you must at least visit your doctor for the two important second and third scans and the last one at 34 weeks. Your doctor will recommend scans on particular dates based on the first scan. Take note that in case there is a report needing urgent attention, an obstetrician can help you only within 20 weeks according to the MTP Act (Amendment 2002)[10].

> The first trimester is crucial to recognise any risk to the pregnancy early.

Ultrasound technology is a very effective tool in detecting complications during pregnancy. For example, ultrasound scans are used along with a blood test called "Dual Marker", between 11 and 13 weeks 6 days to screen for a genetic problem like Down syndrome[11]. Doctors can study the results of this method to also predict other troubling conditions, if any.

It is important to visit the doctor for antenatal check-ups once every month until the seventh month or 30 weeks, thereafter, once every two weeks, transitioning to once every week until delivery. If any complications such as diabetes, high blood pressure or other medical conditions were diagnosed earlier, then plan for more frequent visits for regular monitoring. During these appointments with the doctor, your baseline blood pressure and weight will be recorded and you will be counselled if any high risk factors are detected. Simultaneously, these visits will help you learn how to communicate effectively with your doctor and also understand the process gradually.

Keep note of dates of antenatal check-ups

Fever in pregnancy may be innocuous as in the case of a viral infection or indicative of something that needs immediate attention. So, it is best to be examined even if the fever is mild and let your doctor decide about the course of treatment. Sometimes, the fever may persist with high spikes or be accompanied by a rash. Record your observations and

report any concerns you may have to the doctor.

You are likely to be advised by your doctor to get vaccinated against Tetanus[12], Whooping cough[13] and Diphtheria[14] during pregnancy. In this case, the first dose of vaccination (Td vac) is given around four and a half months into pregnancy, followed by a second dose between the 27th and 36th week. The first dose prevents tetanus and diphtheria; the second dose of vaccination you receive will also include protection against whooping cough in the newborn.

The forthcoming chapters will provide general advice and suggestions to help you get through pregnancy in a healthy and safe way. So, please make yourself comfortable and allot some time to enlighten yourself about the adventure ahead.

Glossary

1. **Ultrasonography:** A diagnostic medical procedure that uses sound waves to produce images of the internal structure of the body on a screen.

2. **Thalassemia:** Inherited blood disorder in which the body makes an abnormal type of haemoglobin.

3. **Thyroid:** The thyroid gland is a butterfly-shaped structure in the front of the neck. The gland uses iodine to produce some vital hormones.

4. **Anaemia:** In the context of this chapter, the type of anaemia referred to is iron-deficiency anaemia, which is more widespread than other types. Iron-deficiency anaemia manifests as weakness resulting from a deficiency of healthy red blood cells needed to carry oxygen to the tissues.

5. **Rubella:** Also known as German Measles, Rubella is a viral infection that can create abnormalities in the foetus if acquired by the pregnant mother.

6. **Diabetes:** A disease in which there is too much sugar in the blood.

7. **Hepatitis B and C:** Viral infections that affect the liver and may be transmitted to the foetus if contracted by a pregnant woman.

8. **Sexually Transmitted Diseases (STDs):** HIV and syphilis are examples of sexually transmitted diseases. Miscarriages and stillbirths are likely when pregnant women contract syphilis.

9. **Electromagnetic radiation:** This is a term that is used to describe a kind of energy that exists all around us in different forms such as radio waves, microwaves, light, and X-rays among others. The Sun and other stars give off electromagnetic radiation.

10. **MTP Act (Amendment 2002):** Abortion law enacted by the Government of India in 1971 to provide termination of pregnancies by registered medical practitioners.

11. **Down syndrome:** A wide range of developmental delays and physical disabilities caused by a genetic disorder.

12. **Tetanus:** Also known as lockjaw, tetanus is a serious bacterial infection that affects the nerves controlling muscle movement, resulting in severe muscle spasms.

13. **Whooping cough:** A highly contagious bacterial infection of the nose and throat. It is also known as pertussis.

14. **Diphtheria:** An infectious, contagious disease which primarily affects the nose and throat.

CHAPTER 3

Unveiling the Mysteries Within

THE AMAZING FACTS about the foetus growing in the womb are so intriguing—I wish I could put my baby back in the womb, and start all over again!

Did you know that your unborn baby has a routine of its own—almost like a mirror image of yours—sleeping, exercising by swimming and somersaulting, eating, swallowing and urinating? (Foetus, however, never defecates unless in distress). Your baby connects to you through its five senses, and imbibes personality traits even while in the womb. If you think personality development is something that happens only at a later stage in life, think again. As a matter of fact, research on the foetus in utero (in the womb) shows that personality development begins before birth, and that there is behavioural continuity from the foetus to the newborn.

Senses and a baby's medium to the world outside the womb

The amniotic fluid is produced by your baby early in pregnancy. During the second trimester of your pregnancy, it acts as a medium through which the baby senses your emotions and behaviours. Amniotic fluid is also the protective medium in which your baby curls up snugly and enjoys the cushioning, warm and sterile environment created by it.

Among the first senses to develop is the sense of touch while your baby explores its own body parts. Senses that develop subsequently are those of taste and smell. Flavours from your diet pass into the amniotic fluid and your baby savours them while swallowing. Julie Mannela (see reference 1), at the Monell Chemical Senses Centre in Philadelphia, USA has conducted research on Prenatal and Postnatal Flavour Learning by Human Infants. According to her

> *Stay calm and stress-free during your pregnancy because your baby can sense your emotions.*

work, "amniotic fluid is a complex first food" that contains chemicals with both taste and smell. Your baby smells and acquires a preference for the scents and flavours of everything you eat, whether it is a carrot, vanilla or garlic.

Research shows that the foetus has a preference for sweet taste, which it indicates by swallowing more amniotic fluid if it tastes sweet. A word of caution here with respect to a pregnant woman consuming sweet supplements for energy: it has been observed that certain influences on the foetus in the womb can have consequences for health in adulthood. For example, a high Body Mass Index or BMI for the mother, and diabetes in pregnancy, can affect the foetal birth weight, from which many diseases can originate and manifest later in life. So, if you are a woman with a high BMI then be aware that you should not be guzzling those litres of Glucon-D.

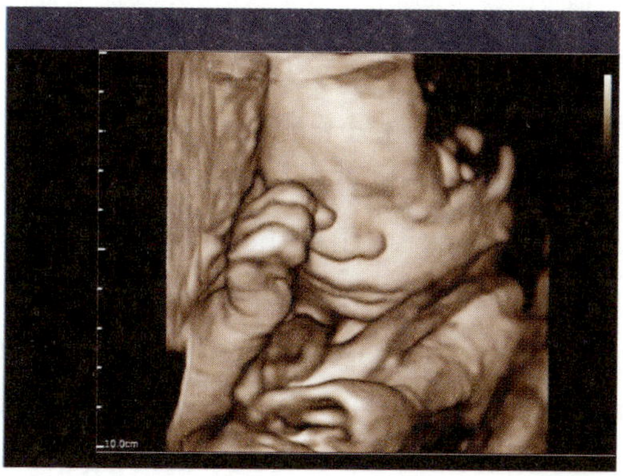

3D image of a baby in the womb – the unknown enigma.

Magnitude and Effects of Sound

Common Examples	dBA	Effect
Breathing	0–10	Hearing threshold
Conversation at home	50–60	Quiet to intrusive
Refrigerator	50	Quiet
Air conditioner	60	Quiet
Shower	70	Annoying
Toilet flushing	75	Annoying
Freeway traffic (15 m), vacuum cleaner, noisy party	70	Annoying, intrusive, possible hearing damage from repeated noise
Watching a movie in a theater, loud vacuum cleaner	85–90	Possible hearing damage from sustained noise
Food processor	95	Damage, if over 1 minute
Jet take-off (at 305 m), motorcycle	100	Damage, if over 1 minute
Thunderclap, textile loom, chain saw, siren, rock concert	120	Human pain threshold
Firecracker	150	Eardrum rupture

Table 3.1 *This table presents notable facts about how sounds emanating from everyday actions and appliances affect hearing. A higher dBA implies greater sound intensity. Data from the World Health Organization and other sources.*

It is a well-established fact that a baby in the womb actually cringes when she/he smells cigarette smoke. The observation is indicative that the unborn baby is able to identify good and bad smells even in the nascent stage.

The sense of hearing is an extensively researched area, particularly the effect of music on the unborn baby. Your baby is quite aware of your voice by the stage of 24 weeks and is conscious of the sound of blood flowing through your blood vessels, sounds of your digestive system, gushing sound of amniotic fluid and your heartbeat. The ideal sound pitch which is comforting to your baby is between 60 and 70 decibels, or dBA[1]. Low-pitched sounds reach the foetus faster than high-pitched sounds, so although a whisper may only be as loud as 30 decibels it will reach the baby more easily than a shrill whistle. Sounds higher than 115 dBA are too loud to be safe around a pregnant woman. Very loud or sudden sounds that startle a pregnant woman can cause changes in her body and affect her growing baby. Besides, these loud sounds can also reach the baby directly through your body. Note that ear muffs can protect the mother but not the baby who will hear the sound as it is. A pregnant mother may unwittingly cause her baby to flutter when using loud home appliances. So, quieter juicers, blenders and washing machines are certainly desirable in the vicinity of a pregnant woman.

Music to your baby's ears

There is a large body of ongoing research about the effects of classical music on the unborn baby. Some Indian classical r*agas* such as *Malkauns*, *Shaant*, *Bageshwari*, *Yaman* and *Bhairav* are especially suitable for pregnant mothers according to eminent classical singer,

Girija Devi (see reference 2, Sumit Jha). Among others, *ragas* such as *Mohanam* and *Madhyamavati* are believed to be calming to the pregnant mother and foetus. In the genre of Western classical music, researchers studied the effect of Mozart's music on the ability to imagine and understand three-dimensional images and shapes, also called "spatial intelligence" and concluded that this kind of intelligence improved temporarily. A theory was built around this finding, termed the Mozart Effect, claiming that exposing infants to classical music is calming and has positive effects on mental evolution. Similarly, the Brahms Lullaby is a German cradle song originally composed by Johannes Brahms, and later sung by many parents to help their babies go to sleep.

> No smoking please because baby doesn't like the smell.
> Avoid noisy surroundings whenever possible.

There is a powerful connection between sound or music and the memory and learning of the unborn baby. This is documented in several articles that describe and discuss research on prenatal music exposure that substantiate the idea that such exposure induces long-term neural[2] effects.

The response to overwhelming sound has also been

studied by Partanen E, Kujala T, Huotilainen M (see reference 3). The heart rate slows down when a mother talks calmly, and increases when the voice is raised. The growing foetus of a mother going through stressful circumstances is exposed to a variety of stress hormones, such as cortisol, which can harm the baby's physical and mental development. So, it is desirable to dwell in calm and musical surroundings. In the same vein, it is wise for any conversations between father and mother to be very pleasant. Further, parents should enjoy regular delightful communication with the unborn baby.

Development of First Foetal Behaviour

Behaviour	Weeks
Just discernible movements	7
Startle	8
Hiccups	9
Breathing movements	10
Hand-to-face contact	10
Yawn	11
Sucking and swallowing	12
Rooting	14
Eye movements	16
Eyes open and blink	26
Facial expressions can be studied using 4D Ultrasonography (see reference 4)	

Table 3.2 ***Source:*** *This table, adapted from www.layyous.com and www.baillement.com/foetal behaviour 2018, describes the gradual development of foetal behaviour over the first twenty-six weeks.*

There is no medical scientific evidence yet that suggests music can mould the personality, but soft, melodious music is certainly a wonderful holistic therapy to soothe the nerves and allow the mother and baby to be peaceful and happy. So let that music play!

Finally, sight is the last sense to develop. Unlike the other senses, sight is not completely evolved in the womb. However, it is known that the eyes can open and close by seven and a half months, and the foetus can even distinguish between light and dark.

Glossary

1. **dB and dBA:** A dB or decibel is the unit used to measure the intensity of sound or loudness. In practice, sound meters are fitted with filters called A-weighting filters when used to measure the relative loudness of different sounds that the human ear hears. When such sound meters are used the units of measurement are referred to as dBA or weighted decibels. The human ear is not very sensitive to sounds below 1000 Hertz in frequency (Hertz is a unit of frequency). As an unweighted meter hears low-frequency sounds louder than the human ear would, the measurement of loudness at these low frequencies is higher in unweighted decibels than in weighted decibels. The A-weighting filter, on the other hand, allows the sound meter to be behave like the human ear when responding to sound frequency. Since the sound the human ear hears is less loud at the low frequencies, the measurement is corrected downwards. For this reason sound levels are measured in dBA.

2. **Neural:** Refers to anything that relates to nerves and the nervous system including the brain and spinal cord.

Yogurt
Milk
Cereal

CHAPTER 4

Nurturing with Nutrition

BEFORE DESIGNING THE meal plan to nourish yourself during pregnancy, please review the following brief primer on the nutritive qualities of various foods.

You have probably come across food guides intending to help create a balanced diet in books and pamphlets on health. Governments in many countries publish guides called "Food Pyramids" which are periodically updated and are accessible at the website of the Food and Agriculture Organization of the United Nations (www.fao.org). A picture or graphical representation of the Indian Food Pyramid can also be viewed at many links in your web browser. In addition, there are links such as, foodpyramidindia.org, that include information on food groups and healthy cooking practices based on diets from different regions in the country. Among other nutrition guides, the most universally known "Food Pyramids" are those published by the United States Department of Agriculture (USDA), the World Health Organization (WHO), and the "Eatwell Plate" from the United Kingdom.

Food Pyramids visually represent the number of servings of foods that should be consumed daily to provide adequate nutrition. Foods are sorted into different groups depending on their nutritive values and properties. Vegetables and fruits, dairy products, grains, beans and legumes, meats, and sugary foods are typical food groups. Water is also included in some definitions.

The food we eat comprises carbohydrates, fats, proteins, fibre, vitamins and minerals that are considered

Source: http://ninindia.org/DietaryGuidelinesforNINwebsite.

necessary for a healthy body. However, to identify what is beneficial for you and what might be detrimental to your health, it is necessary to grasp the sub-classifications of these nutrients to determine whether they are considered 'good' or 'bad' for you. Sub-classifications include simple and complex carbohydrates, saturated, trans and unsaturated fats or soluble and insoluble fibres.

Some carbohydrates such as sugar, candy, unfortified refined flour (*maida*) which is a key ingredient in junk food[1], white bread and white rice are referred to as 'simple' because they are digested quickly. These carbohydrates cause sharp fluctuations in the blood glucose level and tend to encourage overeating. Besides, they have no particular nutritive value. Due to their negative or undesirable properties, the simple carbohydrates are labelled 'bad' or less preferable for health to other foods.

Complex carbohydrates such as fruits and vegetables, cereals and cereal products, including whole wheat

Carbohydrates with high glycaemic index and low glycaemic index.

preparations such as roti and bread, oats and brown rice digest slowly, hence they are a constant source of energy and prevent erratic fluctuations in blood glucose. Unlike simple carbohydrates, complex carbohydrates are considered 'good' for health and their consumption is encouraged. Fruits and vegetables also provide fibre, vitamins and minerals.

Carbohydrates should constitute 45% of the calorie intake of a pregnant woman. This amounts to about 6 to 12 servings in a day where each serving is defined by the type of food. For example, a serving may consist of one roti, one slice of bread, or half a cup of cooked rice. The general rule is to have at least five varieties of fruits and vegetables in a day. Note, dried raisins, dried peas and beans are also included under fruits and vegetables.

Fats should be consumed in moderation. They should comprise less than 30% of the total calorie requirement. Whether fats are classified as 'unsaturated' or 'saturated' depends on their chemical structures. 'Unsaturated fats' are deemed to be 'good' fats, which provide beneficial nutrients to maintain good health. Oils are classified under fats because they have high levels of fat in their composition. Olive oil, peanut oil (for those with no allergy to peanuts), canola oil, soybean oil and sunflower oil are all unsaturated fats.

'Bad' fats are 'saturated fats' and other fats are referred to as 'trans fats'. While saturated fats are needed in moderate quantities, trans fats are to be generally avoided. Ghee, coconut oil, butter and margarine (with no trans fats) are saturated fats. Trans fats like Dalda[2] are found in fried foods and junk foods, so please stay away from them.

Plan meals carefully so you can get enough protein whether you are a vegetarian or non-vegetarian.

Another class of essential nutrients are proteins. A good quality protein is one in which all nine essential amino acids are present, as is readily available in a non-vegetarian diet including lean meats, skinless chicken and freshwater fish. However, due to the presence of a high degree of fat in red meat, its consumption is discouraged. The same quality of protein content may be obtained in a vegetarian meal by combining a variety of plant foods, such as cereals and legumes (*roti/chole*, *rice/rajma* or *dosa/idli* and *sambhar*). Soaked and sprouted mung bean or green gram (*ankurit moong*), mat bean (*moth*)[3] and bengal gram (*chana*) are also recommended as a part of your diet. Milk and milk products are additional sources rich in protein. Remember, being a vegetarian does not mean that you will have an inadequate intake of protein in your diet. So, do not go out of your way to reluctantly start eating eggs or fish if you are unaccustomed to or do not relish eating them.

Fibre may be either soluble or insoluble, based on whether it dissolves in water or not as it passes through the intestines. About 20–25 grams should be included in your daily diet. Fibre, including both soluble and insoluble varieties, is useful to the body in different ways. Soluble fibre digests slowly and allows you to wait for a few hours before your next meal. Insoluble fibre, on the other hand, does not dissolve in or absorb water and is helpful in preventing constipation. Fibre consumption must be spread out during the day because too much of it at a time can cause abdominal discomfort and diarrhoea. Remember to accompany intake of dietary fibre with adequate quantities of water to allow soluble fibre to dissolve in it, once ingested.

Citrus fruits and apricots, vegetables like spinach and broccoli, legumes like peas and beans, and lentils like red lentil (*masoor dal*) and kidney beans (*rajma*) provide the soluble type of fibre. Oats and broken wheat (*dalia*) are high fibre foods. The soluble fibre present in oats helps to keep hunger and blood sugar in check. The fibre in *dalia* prevents constipation and, like oats, it has a low glycaemic index[4] which is particularly helpful for diabetics. Examples of foods containing insoluble fibre are green leafy vegetables, wheat bran as in whole wheat bread or rice bran as in brown rice, and peels of fruits that can be eaten with their skin.

At least four servings of dairy products are desirable daily as they are the richest sources of calcium, a necessary nutrient for good health. Familiar dairy products are double toned and skimmed milk (which has minimal fat but a high calcium content), curd and paneer. For those who are lactose intolerant, there are vegetables that are rich in calcium such as spinach (*palak*), broccoli and lotus stems (*kamal kakdi*). In case you tolerate lactose-free milk you might consider trying some if it is available where you live. Other sources of calcium are nuts like almonds (*badam*) and buttermilk (*chaas*).

There has been some debate over the issue of whether almonds should be consumed dry or after being soaked overnight and peeled. Certain substances that are present in the skin of almonds cause difficulty in digestion for some. For people who suffer from such indigestion, soaking and peeling the skin gets rid of these substances, thereby allowing proper absorption of all the nutrients that almonds have to offer, making this a better way to eat them.

Other vital nutrients are vitamins and minerals which are present in almost all fruits and vegetables. Folic acid, iron, calcium and vitamin D3 are absolutely essential. Also necessary are minerals like copper, zinc and choline. Tofu (*soya milk paneer*), bottle gourd (*lauki*) and peanuts are sources that are rich in folic acid. Foods loaded in iron are spinach, fenugreek (*methi*), dates (*khajur*), figs (*anjeer*), pomegranate (*anar*), beetroot and apple to quote a few.

> Eat 5 varieties of fruits and vegetables daily if you can.

Docosahexaenoic Acid[5] (DHA) is an essential fatty acid which must be included in the meal plan, as it plays an important role in brain development of the growing foetus (baby in the womb). Seafood and eggs are rich sources of DHA. However, vegetarians can obtain DHA from seeds, nuts and beans, green leafy vegetables and some oils. Notable sources are flaxseeds, walnuts, mung, navy and pinto beans, soy foods, kidney beans (*rajma*), green leafy vegetables, cabbage, olive and canola oils.

Notes for nutrition

Now that you are armed with the basics of healthful nutrients and a sample of easily accessible sources, you can draw up a daily or weekly meal plan for yourself. Before drawing up the plan, you must become familiar with the framework within which to organise the intake of nutrient rich foods. For this, you may keep a couple of dictums in mind. Once you create the plan, these same meals must be healthy for the rest of the family too.

Secondly, as some vitamins are lost in cooking water, use this water elsewhere instead of discarding it; alternatively, you can cook vegetables using the minimum quantity of water needed without burning them.

Eat frequent small meals which are approximately 2 to 3 hours apart. This can be achieved by including three main courses comprising breakfast, lunch and dinner as anchors and introducing small wholesome snacks in between. The main courses should consist of one or two servings of all the major food groups discussed above. Snacks can consist of whole fruit such as kiwi, citrus, apple and other seasonal varieties. Try to consume fruit by eating them rather than drinking them in the form of juice. Whenever possible eat the peels as they

Healthy morning snack.

contain additional nutrition. The rind of an orange can be grated and added to your cereal. Fresh, washed and well-prepared salads may be had without dressings. Milk or buttermilk may be blended with fruits like bananas, apples or mangoes to make delicious milk shakes and smoothies.

Hydrate yourself with coconut water, lemon water, Indian style buttermilk (*chaas*), or plain and purified (filtered or boiled) water. Read labels when purchasing Tetra Paks to ensure that they contain 100% juice and not a diluted variety or one containing artificial sweeteners. Stay away from soft drinks that contain unhealthy artificial flavourings and preservatives. Avoid colas because they contain caffeine, which can decrease blood flow to the placenta[6] and affect the growing baby. Caffeine also acts like a diuretic (causing one to pass excess urine) leading to loss of fluid or dehydration. Note that diet sodas may contain artificial sweeteners.

A useful piece of information is that calcium reduces the absorption of iron, so combining calcium rich foods with iron rich foods is not a good idea. On the other hand, vitamin C enhances the absorption of iron. To illustrate, both calcium and iron are already present in spinach which is a regularly consumed source of iron. Since spinach is a natural food, they exist in forms that the body can absorb. However, it is best not to drink a glass of milk following a corn and spinach sandwich because the calcium in the milk prevents efficient absorption of iron from spinach. To boost iron absorption, try to combine an iron rich food, like the spinach sandwich, with a glass of orange or lemon juice instead of milk. The orange or lemon juice should preferably be taken just before an iron-rich meal to encourage complete iron absorption. Likewise, if taking an iron supplement, do so before a meal containing vitamin C foods.

Foods to avoid

While we have reviewed healthy foods, there are some foods that must be eaten in moderation or avoided altogether during pregnancy. Seafood is suspected to have a high content of mercury because fish ingest it from industrial waste. If you are confident about the source and wish to eat seafood, salmon, catfish, and sardines may be safe provided one is not allergic to them. Incidentally, the presence of vitamin A in cod liver oil is too high to be safe for the baby, so pregnant women are dissuaded from consuming it in any form. Blue cheese, which is old fermented cheese, may be avoided, while processed cheese slices and mozzarella are safe. Pregnant women tend to consume saffron (*kesar*) believing it will give the baby a fair and glowing complexion. We do not have adequate evidence regarding its safety or of its role in the skin-related myth. What we do know is that, if eaten, it should be in minute quantities, preferably after the fifth month, as large amounts can encourage a miscarriage[7]. Half cooked meats or salads containing raw meats are not recommended as they can lead to an infection called *toxoplasmosis*[8]. Refrigerated, smoked seafood or unpasteurized milk can cause an infection called *listeriosis*[9]. If you are accustomed to drinking coffee, you may consume up to 200 mgs, preferably less than 100 mgs, of caffeine per day (1 cup of instant coffee contains 75 mgs of caffeine and one cup of tea contains 45 to 50 mgs of caffeine). It is believed that too much caffeine restricts blood flow to the foetus and inhibits growth, although there is yet no hard evidence to confirm this (American College of Obstetricians and Gynecologists or ACOG, 2010)[1]. If you wish to consume flaxseeds, do so in moderation. Junk foods are high in sugar, salt and calories with little nutritive value. Instant foods have additives whose safety is questionable. Artificial sweeteners like saccharin must be shunned although sweeteners containing aspartame and sucralose can be had in moderation (read labels).

Take steps to maintain good hygiene when cooking and consuming food. Be sure to wash vegetables well to remove harmful pesticides and other chemical residue. Steer clear of street foods and, as far as possible, eat at home and give up the temptation to eat out.

> *Enjoy frequent small meals approximately 2-3 hours apart.*

Some women suffer from Pica, which is an unnatural urge to eat stuff like chalk, sand, mud, clay or ash. This has to be curbed and cured as it can prove to be dangerous. Consult your doctor as this is generally due to iron deficiency or anaemia. Chewing sugarless gum might help during such cravings.

Finally, once your intelligently designed meal planner is ready, you should do justice to the prepared meal. This means you must endeavour to have your meal on time. Begin with an early breakfast after your unintentional overnight fast. Find time to enjoy the meal by taking a break of at least 30 minutes, whether at home or at work. Do not try to multitask at the same time. Focus on your food, chew well and relish every morsel. Give wholehearted attention to your meal and you will find that you have digested the meal better. End the meal with plenty of water after a gap of about twenty minutes to help with digestion.

Eating right is important during pregnancy. You may create a very well-thought out meal planner based on the primer in this chapter. In addition, it is wise to consult a dietician who will recommend a diet plan for you that is individualised depending on various factors like your body weight, history of diabetes and iron deficiency. In a woman with a normal BMI, calorie intake should range anywhere between 1800 to 2200 calories per day. This is to say that a normal, healthy calorie intake is sufficient in the first trimester. During the second and third trimesters, an additional 300–350 calories per day are required.

Food	Grams of Protein	Calories
1 cup of whole milk	8	149
1 cup of chopped broccoli	3	31
1 cup of boiled lentils	18	230
1 ounce or a serving of 28 grams of almonds	6	161
1 large egg	6	78
1 roasted chicken breast without skin	53	284
½ cup of raw oats	6	303
1 cup of paneer or cottage cheese with 2% fat	27	194
3 ounces of fresh water fish	19	175
1 ounce or 28 grams of peanuts	7	159
1 cup of cooked green peas	9	134
1 cup or 240 ml of soy milk	7	129
1 cup of cooked spinach or broccoli	4-5	23
1 cup of skimmed milk	8.5	86
1 cup of lowfat yogurt (curd)	14	137

Table 4.1 *Protein content and the number of calories provided by various routinely consumed foods. This table is of particular use to vegetarians to assess if their protein and calorie intake is adequate in each trimester of pregnancy. (1 cup=8 fl. ounces or 237 ml of liquid. In practice, a 240 ml cup is used to measure dry goods).*

Glossary

1. **Junk food:** Foods that have a high content of sugar, salt, trans fats and undesirable, empty calories. Such foods tend to contain plain flour or white flour (*maida*) and sugar among key ingredients. Examples are milk bread, fruit bread, pizza and burgers.

2. **Dalda:** A familiar brand of hydrogenated vegetable oil used in cooking.

3. **Moth:** Also known as *matki*, is a kind of bean or dal that looks like brown moong dal in appearance.

4. **Glycaemic index:** Carbohydrates break down into a sugar called glucose. The glycaemic index of a given carbohydrate is a number that ranks how quickly and by how much the body breaks it down into glucose thus expressing the relative ability of the carbohydrate in a specific food to increase the level of glucose in the blood.

5. **Docosahexaenoic Acid (DHA):** An omega-3 fatty acid necessary for growth and functional development of the brain.

6. **Placenta:** A flattened circular organ that is filled with blood vessels. It is attached to the uterus on one side and provides nutrients and oxygen to the baby through the umbilical cord, which is attached to its inner surface.

7. **Miscarriage:** Also called abortion, it means the loss of a pregnancy before 20 weeks.

8. **Toxoplasmosis:** A parasitic infection acquired by eating partly cooked meat and from contact with cats and their faeces or stools.

9. **Listeriosis:** Foodborne bacterial infection caused by eating contaminated food. It can be very serious for pregnant women as their immunity can be low or impaired.

CHAPTER 5

Challenges to a Beautiful Pregnancy

EVERY PREGNANT WOMAN exudes a radiant glow. Soon, however, even as the new reality brought home by the positive pregnancy test sinks in, certain changes in the body begin to appear that may cause some worry. But, feeling good during pregnancy is of pivotal importance. A baby whose mother is full of vitality senses the positive vibes coming from all those steps she takes to look beautiful and feel great. So, although concern due to the physical transformation can be distressing, you should continue to face the challenge and look after yourself. Luckily, the silver lining is that the changes that occur tend to fade with time, after delivery.

There are a number of alterations in your face and body during pregnancy, which may raise questions in your mind about the ways in which to care for them and their associated consequences. Some of the changes that may be observed are:

- Facial discolouration that can cause the skin to turn dark and patchy, with patches showing especially on the cheeks and forehead. The appearance of these marks is called *chloasma* or "the mask of pregnancy" and arises due to an increased secretion of a pigment called melanin.

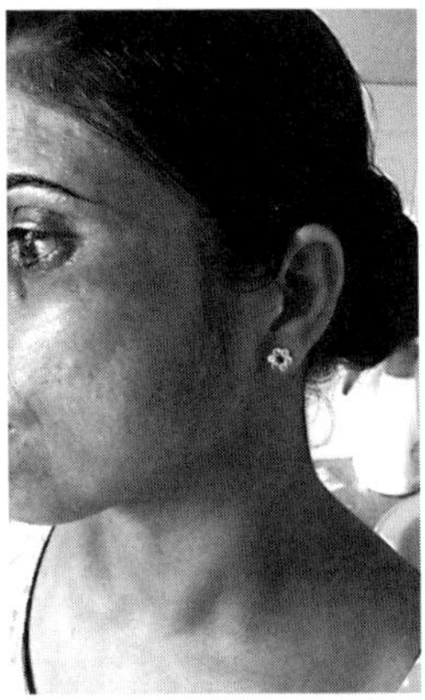

Chloasma, a patchy effect of melanin pigment.

- The skin may become either too dry or too oily, resulting in dandruff or acne.
- Pregnancy leads to weight gain, which in turn physically stretches the skin. In addition, certain hormones cause water retention in the skin, thus weakening and disrupting collagen and elastic fibre between cells. These changes may appear as stretch marks or striae on the stomach, breasts and thighs.
- A dark line like a winding trail, called the linea

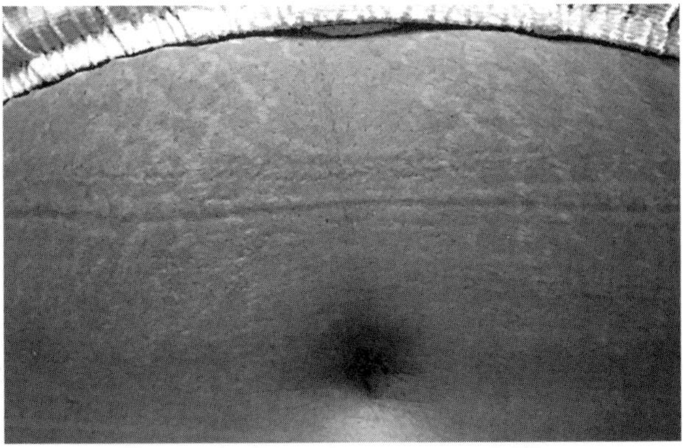

Stretch marks in pregnancy (Striae gravidarum).

nigra, may appear in the middle of the tummy around the fifth month in first pregnancies. It may show up earlier than the fifth month in subsequent pregnancies. Starting from the navel, the trail runs downwards and gets darker as the pregnancy advances. Sometimes, it may also extend upwards beyond the navel.

- As a pregnant woman, you may have a waddling gait. This "duck walk" happens due to a shift in the centre of gravity.
- Ankles and feet may swell to a point where it becomes difficult to distinguish between them and the calves. This kind of swelling is called edema or oedema.
- You may suffer from poor digestion and increased gas, acidity and constipation.

The physiological changes that manifest in pregnancy are due to increased levels of the hormones, estrogen and progesterone, and also because of a pigment called melanin. The most important message to focus on is that the changes are natural. So, think of them as charming milestones that are an integral part of your beautiful journey through pregnancy.

Besides, you may observe some positive signs that appear along the way. Thank the pregnancy hormones for that gorgeous glow throughout and the crowning glory of lovely, thick hair. In fact, the hair remains in its growing phase for a longer time than normal and sheds only after delivery.

If you confront any of the more annoying changes and are looking for simple, safe ways to tackle them, read on. However, be wary as there is no evidence-based research that indicates what is absolutely safe or unsafe. You are advised to proceed after observing the points in the following message of caution.

Note of caution

Consult your doctor if you observe the following changes:

- Increase in ankle swelling or general puffiness
- Breathlessness
- Excess weight gain

All of the above symptoms can unmask occult (not visible to the eye) medical complications of pregnancy.

Home remedies for a glowing skin

Regular washing of face and hands should be at the top of your list of home remedies. Hands and nails devoid of grease and dust keep pimples at bay.

There are a number of remedies to address changes in skin tone or texture. If you suffer from dry and dehydrated skin, reach for some yogurt. Curd can be very effective in treating dull and dry skin. Apply it on the face, leave it on for half an hour and rinse it off to look and feel fresh. Needless to state that consuming curd also nourishes the skin, so go ahead and make it a part of your diet in the form of smoothies, *raita* or in any other healthy recipe.

If, on the other hand, your skin is too oily due to overactive sebaceous glands[1], then you can try using ripe papaya pulp, or a mixture of gram flour (*besan*)), milk and turmeric as a face pack. A mixture of honey and lime juice can also work wonders on an oily skin. Another option for a face pack is a paste made from neem (*Azadirachta indica*), mint and sacred basil (*tulsi*)) leaves.

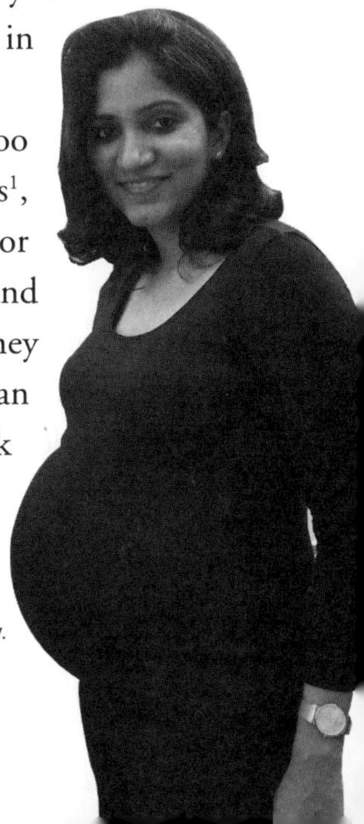

Growing pregnancy.

Stretch marks may be smoothened by gently applying cocoa butter creams and vitamin E oil in a circular manner on the tummy and breasts. Gently massage the nipples in an outward direction in preparation for breastfeeding after delivery. Vigorous massaging of the breast and nipple with the cream can stimulate uterine contractions, so do not overdo it.

Changes like facial discolouration and striae are normal and fade away or reduce after delivery.

Yoga has a lot to offer to keep the body supple and healthy during pregnancy. *Asanas*, such as *Vajrasana* (Diamond pose), *Titli Asana* (Butterfly pose) and *Sukhasana* (Easy pose) can be done to decrease stress and improve muscle tone. Yoga can also help to reduce stretch marks in the process.

The simplest and most effective of all items on the to-do list is to follow a healthy diet. Eat and drink in a wholesome way. Your diet should be rich in protein, include homemade vegetable soups and juices, coconut water and plenty of fruits. We have already discussed the need to chart out a healthy diet in chapter 4.

If you are someone who likes to visit the beauty parlour to pamper yourself, consult your doctor before venturing into it for any advice pertaining to your specific case. Generally, you may continue to do so, provided you bear the following principles in mind:

> Wash hands and face clean to maintain your glow.
> Adequate hydration and a healthy diet are key to maintaining your vitality.

- Select a parlour that is well-ventilated and uncrowded and has staff trained in treating a pregnant woman.
- Remember that increased inhalation of chemicals can cause breathlessness.
- Threading and waxing on the face and arms are safe, preferably with your own wax, as parlour wax is shared among several clients. Avoid waxing on the abdomen and in the bikini area.

Hair care

Use only mild shampoos and ammonia-free hair dyes. According to the American College of Obstetricians and Gynaecologists[1] (ACOG), hair dyes are probably safe to use during pregnancy because very small amounts of dyes are absorbed through the skin. However, it is important to be cautious and limit their use. Avoid the "hair rebonding" procedure while still pregnant.

Skin care

The only safe way to address *chloasma* is by camouflaging it with make-up and avoiding excessive exposure to the sun. Use a sunscreen cream or lotion with an SPF rating of at least 15. Read labels and refrain from applying ointments containing tretinoin on the skin. Use those containing hydroquinone sparingly.

Gentle and basic facials, which do not include blackhead removal or passing electric current are acceptable. Chemical peels are not advisable.

Do not get into saunas and hot tub baths, especially during the first trimester. An increase in core body temperature can result in Spina bifida[2] in the baby, which is an abnormality of the spine.

But above all, remember that all the changes that take place on your face and body are a natural part of your pregnancy, and are beautiful. Be extra cautious with treatments during this phase and do not experiment. Simple steps can make you feel great and exude confidence. Spoil yourself with a new wardrobe of airy and comfortable clothes and shoes. Maybe even get a new look by changing your hairstyle.

Famous Russian thinker and author Leo Tolstoy said, “If you want to be happy, be”. Likewise, if you are pregnant and want to be beautiful, be!

Glossary

1. **Sebaceous glands:** Small groups of cells in the skin that produce oily substances to smoothen hair and skin.

2. **Spina bifida:** Abnormal development of the spine.

CHAPTER 6

Working while Pregnant

A LARGE NUMBER of pregnant women in India are engaged in demanding occupations, often juggling housework and professional employment. Some of them choose to pursue a career out of choice, while others do it to supplement their family earnings. Likewise, a pregnant homemaker may be single-handedly attending to all household chores. Whatever the reason, pregnant women engaged in strenuous activity will face challenges along the way. If your doctor allows you to continue working, then she/he has probably determined that your pregnancy is free of risk.

The prepared, pregnant office-goer.

Dealing with the annoyances of pregnancy alongside office work can be stressful in itself. If household chores are also added to the daily agenda, then you are inviting trouble. Get your priorities right and plan ahead to arrange for help with household work. You should re-evaluate your work profile because working with the same degree of enthusiasm and drive, as you did prior to pregnancy, might be difficult. There may be hurdles that you have to overcome that can arise due to pregnancy or due to the nature of the job or both.

The distressing features of pregnancy occur in phases. Nausea and vomiting happen in the first trimester, referring to the first three months; fatigue, swollen feet, and occasional urinary leaks manifest in the third trimester or the last three months. The middle phase, which is the second trimester, can be considered the honeymoon phase because your appetite improves and you begin to feel more energetic. Further, in a healthy pregnancy, you are not hampered by restrictions on active leisure and travel in the second trimester as you are in the first and third trimesters.

Gear up for the challenges

To prepare for the challenges ahead, begin by improving your level of physical comfort in the workplace. This includes using a straight-backed chair, a cushion for your back and a stool to keep your feet raised while you work. The height of your chair should be such that your hands are at the level of the keyboard if using one. Arranging the height in this way reduces the risk of suffering from Carpal Tunnel Syndrome[1]. Keep a bottle of water handy as a reminder to hydrate yourself well. As small meals are highly desirable, keep small containers of snacks within reach. I suggest fruits, nuts, salads, sprouts and a bottle of *lassi* or buttermilk, lemon juice or coconut water.

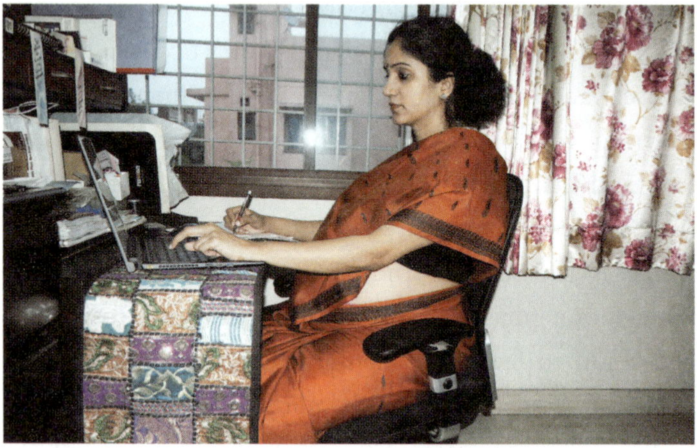

Note the straight backed chair and the arms resting on the table at the level of the keyboard. Feet can be put up on a stool or the UPS!

It is in your interest to be pragmatic. Approach your Human Resources Department and learn about office or company policies for pregnant employees, maternity benefits, insurance and options for flexible working hours. Also, enquire about your ability to work from home, which may be useful in the last month of pregnancy. If your work is accompanied by occupational hazards, such as exposure to chemicals, fumes or radiation, you must find out about policies to protect pregnant women. It may even be possible to get reassigned to a different, less risky task, while pregnant.

Analyse your means of transport as at no point should there be any element of hurry. If travelling by car, leave early to avoid fast driving or the need for sudden application of brakes. Do not hesitate to use the seat belt (see image below). Avoid an overcrowded bus, metro train or local train and try to catch the next one, if possible.

Travelling by air when pregnant

Physiological effects on the mother and environmental influences on both mother and baby are important concerns to a pregnant woman embarking on air travel.

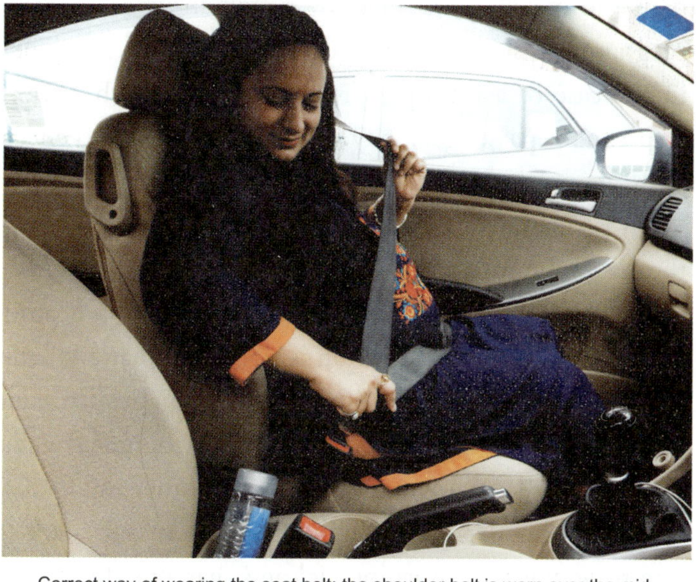

Correct way of wearing the seat belt: the shoulder belt is worn over the mid-shoulder, then mid-chest and over the top of the pregnancy. The lap portion of the belt is placed below the pregnancy. Move seat back away from steering wheel and tilt steering wheel towards the face and not the pregnancy.

> If pursuing a career, prepare ahead to strike a balance between office work and housework.

The airline industry acknowledges the risk of premature labour pains that a pregnant woman can suffer while in transit. As a pregnant passenger who has completed 28 weeks, you would be required to provide certification by your doctor stating that you are fit to travel. Generally, many airlines ban air travel by a woman whose normal pregnancy has crossed the 36-week mark and 32 weeks in the case of a multiple pregnancy. Rules with respect to pregnant passengers may vary across airlines, so check with the specific airline you are booked on before travel.

It is believed that the high altitude of the cabin lowers the saturation level of oxygen in the blood by 10% of the total. The reduction has little consequence for a healthy woman. Even cosmic radiation is not problematic as long as you don't travel by air often, as say a flight attendant does. Any radiation from body scanners, encountered when checking in, also does not pose a risk to mother and foetus.

However, not surprisingly, discomfort can be felt due to aggravated morning sickness, gaseous distension and earache from nasal congestion. These annoyances are minor compared to the risk posed by Deep Vein Thrombosis[2] (DVT), especially in those who are already at high risk. Individuals with a family history of DVTs or who have had a previous episode of DVT, or who have a high Body Mass Index (BMI) are all potentially at high risk for DVT. So, if travel is longer than 3 to 4 hours, it is vital that you adhere to the following guidelines to minimise the risk of DVT:

- Take an aisle seat to facilitate ease of movement.
- Walk regularly and do some exercises while seated. Keep yourself well-hydrated but avoid caffeine and alcohol.
- Special GE[3] stockings may have to be worn for very long distance travel.

Your doctor may discourage air travel under certain circumstances, such as, if your haemoglobin[4] (Hb) is below 7.5 gms or if you had a recent episode of bleeding. Other roadblocks can be a middle ear infection or sinusitis, recent sickle crisis, serious heart or respiratory disease, recent surgical treatment for gastrointestinal issues, or a fractured leg in a cast that can result in swelling due to immobility during air travel.

In early pregnancy, it is best to confirm the presence of a live pregnancy (in the uterus) by an ultrasound test before proceeding to travel. Carry a copy of your medical records and any documents relating to travel insurance, ensuring that the insurance covers pregnancy. While seated on the aircraft, remember to fasten your seatbelt below your abdomen, on the lap. If you need to be vaccinated before travelling, make sure the vaccine is the inactivated type.

Food goodie bag suggestions

- Seasonal fruit
- Soup, yogurt, *lassi*, buttermilk, fresh juice, or coconut water
- Corn and spinach sandwich with multigrain bread or peanut butter sandwich (for those not allergic to peanuts), or hot *idlis* with *chutney*
- Dry fruits
- Flattened rice (*poha*) with seasonal vegetables
- Hygienically prepared sprout salads
- Homemade hummus (soaked chickpeas or *kabuli chana* cooked and ground with a dash of lemon juice, a very small quantity of sesame seeds, olive oil, garlic, water and salt). Indians generally discourage sesame seeds during pregnancy although there is no scientific evidence to support this view. Some prefer to remove the skin from the boiled *chana* before grinding them in the blender, for a smoother consistency.

Preventives and precautions

- For handling nausea:
    - Ginger tea and crackers
- For handling fatigue:
    - Take short breaks, hydrate, consume iron-rich foods
- To cut back on activities
    - Shop online
    - Hire maid
    - Take the help of friends or helpful neighbours for small errands, like buying groceries and cleaning supplies
- While bending do so by bending at the knees, not at your waist
- While lifting use your legs (see figure 1) and not your back
- Follow your fitness regime, but be cautious and avoid too much stress
- Most important of all sleep early to wake up feeling energetic and refreshed. If possible, add a short power nap during breaks.

Follow dos and don'ts prescribed by your doctor, eg. avoid lifting heavy weights.

Dos and Don'ts: In Your Role as a Professional

- Always make sure you are well hydrated; have small meals often and take short breaks when feasible.
- If your job involves standing all the time, remember to sit down on and off; stand if you are sitting all the time. Walk around from time to time to maintain blood circulation and keep the muscles flexible and exercised. In the third trimester, try to take an occasional day off and de-stress during the weekends. Most women try to work till the date of delivery in order to save "leave days" for the post-delivery period. But it's important to know your limits and take the last few weeks off, especially if it involves travelling long distances to the office or venue.
- Finally, try to complete and organise your file work for a pleasant handing over.

Dos and Don'ts: In Your Role as a Homemaker

- Get furniture rearranged and remove superfluous decorative rugs and mats to prevent tripping.
- Lifting heavy objects is out of the question when you are pregnant. Hence, guard against a natural tendency to lift a bucket of water or clothes to be dried. Avoid picking up even the pressure cooker!

- It is strange but true that the pregnant woman feels an urge to indulge in spring cleaning and cleaning in general, believing that it will help to have a "normal delivery". Washing toilets, sweeping and mopping floors are among the activities that a pregnant woman tends to want to do. However, beware of accidents arising due to losing your balance or tripping over something that can cause bleeding or premature pains. So, be sensible about cleaning projects, especially those involving lifting heavy objects. Even if it is something you always do, it is prudent to remain cautious.
- Eat small meals periodically, be well hydrated and catch up on an afternoon nap.
- It is important to walk for at least 30 minutes every day or at least three to four times a week.

Note of caution

- Do not skip regular antenatal check-ups.
- Poor weight gain, restricted growth of the baby, or a mild rise in blood pressure are indications that you should be resting at home.

Working during pregnancy is a boon financially, and a major distraction from the discomforts of the big belly,

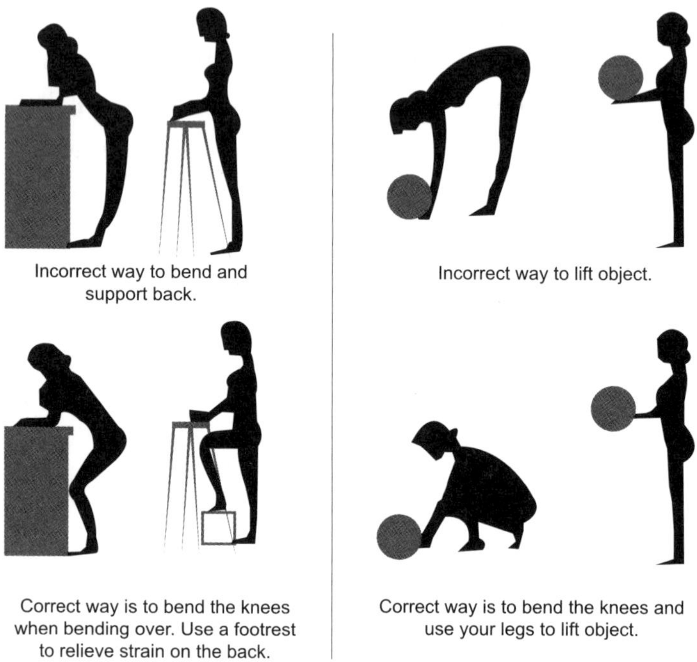

Figure 1

but a bane if problems set in. Be sure to plan ahead to get help, and follow all that has been advised so far in order to overcome the obstacles you face, whether working at the office or at home. As a primer, remember to attend antenatal check-ups, make yourself comfortable at work, avoid lifting heavy weights, have small meals frequently, stay hydrated and incorporate light exercise such as walking every day.

Glossary

1. **Carpal Tunnel Syndrome:** Pressure on the median nerve to the palm leading to tingling, numbness and pain in all the fingers except the little finger.

2. **Deep Vein Thrombosis (DVT):** Also known as economy-class syndrome, DVT refers to a blood clot in a deep vein in the leg or thigh. The risk of forming a blood clot, as in DVT, is widely known to exist when travelling by air, particularly in the economy class where passengers are in very cramped positions for many hours. For this reason, passengers on long-distance flights are encouraged to walk in the aisles and exercise their limbs from time to time, even while seated. DVT can result in any kind of travel involving prolonged sitting causing immobility.

3. **GE:** Graduated Elastic also known as Graduated Compression Stockings

4. **Haemoglobin (Hb):** A protein in the red blood cells which carries oxygen throughout the body.

CHAPTER 7

Mild to Moderate Workouts, not Burnouts

DO YOU SUBSCRIBE to the notion that it is a pregnant woman's prerogative to be a couch potato? It is time to change that mindset. Perhaps you may feel overwhelmed by the conflicting advice about exercise you receive from many fronts. Rest assured, however, that there is ample evidence to show that mild to moderate exercise is in fact beneficial to healthy, pregnant women in many ways.

The question then is "What is mild to moderate exercise for any given individual?" The intensity of exercise largely depends on a variety of factors. They include whether or not you were exercising before you became pregnant, your current Body Mass Index[1] (BMI) and your pregnancy status, specifically, whether you are in a high or low risk situation. Even if you are an amateur, there is no cause for concern because there are a variety of exercise options to help you initiate your desired fitness program. Always start slowly and gradually increase to moderate intensity. As far as weight is concerned, an increase of 12 to 14 kilos over the entire pregnancy is considered normal. However, if you have a high BMI, then you should modify your diet and exercise to target a gain of only 8 to 10 kilos of overall body weight. Note: the suggestion is to watch what you eat and not start dieting! If your pregnancy is classified as high risk, then make sure to consult your doctor before contemplating exercise of any intensity.

As stated earlier, exercise is beneficial in pregnancy. But why? Have you heard of the "Happy Hormones"? Endorphins, the feel good hormones that are released when you exercise, work to reduce your anxiety and sensitivity to pain. So, what better way to prepare for labour and birth? Exercise helps to overcome pain by promoting muscle strength and stamina. Deep breathing techniques like Lamaze[2], yoga and Hypnobirthing[3] are positive contributors to building up a woman's confidence in her ability to give birth. Although there is no scientific evidence, professionals who provide training in specialised breathing techniques, as in certain types of

Class for antenatal and postnatal exercises.

yoga, point to the beneficial effect of deep breathing on pain relief even to the extent that an epidural injection[4] may not be necessary.

Exercise is a stress buster. It will help you sleep better. Exercise also decreases any feeling of bloatedness and relieves constipation. Backache is relieved by doing specific exercises to strengthen the muscles that support the spine. Exercise will control weight gain and there is evidence that it can reduce the risk of certain pregnancy complications like gestational diabetes[5] and preeclampsia[6]. In any form of exercise, movements involving lying on your back must be avoided from the second trimester onwards. This is because the growing belly presses on the major blood vessels below it, thereby decreasing the blood supply to the uterus, simultaneously making you uncomfortable and breathless. Make sure you have a trained instructor, who is aware of exercises specifically designed to protect your back in the antenatal and postnatal phases of pregnancy. It is important for you to continue to do the exercises at home as instructed in the class. Perhaps your husband can also join you.

Workout wonders

The key to a workout recommended for pregnant women is that they should maintain their balance and focus on 'low impact' movements. These consist of exercises designed to protect the joints and musculoskeletal tissues from too much stress, in order to prevent injury. However mild these exercises may seem, they can strengthen and improve muscle flexibility in spite of being low impact routines. Regular walking and swimming are exercises that increase one's breathing and heart rates. Stationary cycling reduces the risk of falling off when pregnant, as compared to riding an outdoor bike. Low impact aerobics[7] strengthen the cardiovascular system. Other low impact pursuits may be modified yoga and relaxation exercises, light weight resistance[8] exercises, general stretching and Pilates[9]. Also note Kegel pelvic floor exercises[10] and water aerobics assist in strengthening muscles. Workouts based on the Lamaze philosophy of birth help to improve breath control. If you are a regular runner or a gym freak, you can continue the same routine when pregnant but with reduced intensity. Choose the workout that suits your body type and that you find appealing.

On the home front, continuing to do some house work is a form of exercise. Light gardening, cleaning, and indulging in small tasks like laying and clearing the table are all activities that exercise the body. However, as advised with low impact exercises, do not attempt chores that can make you lose your balance.

Homemaker carrying on usual chores—cooking.

Homemaker carrying on usual chores—gardening.

The American College of Obstetricians and Gynaecologists (ACOG) recommends 30 minutes of exercise per day, at least 3 to 4 times a week. On a scale of 10, the level of exertion should be between 5 and 6, according to American College of Sports Medicine (ACSM).

There are certain precautions that need to be taken to prepare for your exercise regimen as a pregnant woman—even if it is just walking. First and foremost, get a clearance from your doctor. Wear comfortable clothing and footwear. Make sure you warm up before you exercise and cool off after you finish your routine. Keep sipping water at regular intervals and remain hydrated. Naturally, your nutritional needs will increase during pregnancy.

Listen to your body and recognise your limitations. Remember the Talk Test to keep your exercise intensity in check. This test says that you should be able to hold a normal conversation while exercising. Do not push from enjoyable to exasperating because that increases the core body temperature to unsafe levels.

Walking briskly and general stretching are simple, safe exercises. All that is required is a brisk walk for 30 minutes daily or for most days in a week. You may run at a moderate pace only if you were a regular runner before. You can even do upper arm exercises at home while watching television and shed some excess calories.

Refrain from contact sports, such as kabaddi and hockey. Also, stay away from sports like horse riding and skiing where there is a higher probability of losing your balance as compared to other options. Scuba-diving and sports which require one to lie on the back for long stretches of time are also not recommended. Most important of all, avoid exercising in hot, humid weather.

Swimming

Swimming is an exceptionally good and enjoyable exercise in pregnancy. It strengthens and tones your muscles and because of the gravity free-environment, you are relieved of the weight of your big belly while exercising. Swimming is an excellent way to get blood circulation going. In the first three months, you can swim using any of the different strokes. But from the second trimester onwards, it is advisable to avoid the backstroke, in spite of buoyancy while swimming. Non-swimmers can take up water aerobics, which is a good form of exercise and can be done in the shallow end of the pool. There is some concern regarding the presence of chlorine in the swimming pool. It is believed that the greatest risk in swimming pools arises from chloroform, which can result from a chemical reaction between chlorine, dead skin cells and residues of shampoo and body-care products. There is yet no evidence on which this belief is based. Hence the overall benefits of swimming outweigh the risks, at present. To be on the safe side, however, you can take precautionary measures to minimise exposure to chloroform. Wearing a cap and showering before getting into the pool are customarily practised protective methods. They are effective to a large extent because the cap limits water contamination due to hair-care products and showering removes dead skin cells needed to produce chloroform. Preferably, avoid

Walk, swim or do yoga cautiously after consulting your doctor.

swimming in public pools, if possible.

Swimming as an exercise is not easily accessible to everyone considering the high cost of membership to private pools and clubs. Thus, a large number of Indian women prefer other modes of exercise to swimming.

Yoga

Indian women share the universal appeal of yoga, a set of practices rooted in Hindu Vedic texts from ancient times in India. As a form of exercise that is relatively inexpensive

Yoga—calming and relaxing and at the same time strengthening the muscles.

to pursue, it is a popular alternative to swimming. Practising yoga not only alleviates some health concerns, reduces stress and makes the spine supple, but also boosts blood circulation during pregnancy. It is easy for women who have already been practising yoga to continue exercising while pregnant. Those who plan to take up yoga during pregnancy can do so in the second trimester. It is advisable to avoid *yogasanas* in the first trimester, as they can be tiring for some women. According to the British Wheel of Yoga[1], there is no evidence to suggest that yoga causes miscarriage.

Exercise for my baby's health and mine

Pregnancy is not a sickness so be active and don't be a couch potato.

Yoga may be safely practised in the second trimester, noting that *yogasanas* including forms of *Sarvangasana, Ananda Balasana, Pavan Muktasana, Padottasana,* etc. are among those that are not recommended for pregnant women as they involve lying on the back. The final *Savasana,* when one relaxes after a yoga session, is modified after 20 weeks of pregnancy, so that you lie sideways to avoid pressure on the back and the major blood vessels. Pillows can be placed between the knees for support. For some postures, the instructor may ask you to perform yogic exercises against a wall to prevent slouching. Perform sitting *asanas* on the sitting bones and not on the tailbone. You can do so by placing a cushion under the tail bone. Ligaments and joints get lax in pregnancy due to the pregnancy hormone, Relaxin. Yoga and all other exercises help to strengthen them. One great benefit of yoga, versus other forms of exercise, is that it leaves you with a sense of peace and calm. Deep breathing in yoga and meditation helps you connect with your baby. There are many *asanas*, such as, *Trikonasana and Utthita Parsvakonasana,* that are especially beneficial during pregnancy. Their suitability will depend on the trimester in question. However, avoid *asanas* with strong backbends, or those involving balancing postures or requiring the strong use of abdominal muscles. The body inverting *asanas*, like the head and shoulder stands (*Salamba Sarvangasana* and *Sarvangasana*), are obviously absolutely unacceptable.

The *Pranayamas* or breathing techniques are central to yoga. Breath awareness is fundamental to all yoga childbirth classes or Prenatal Yoga. When the time comes to deliver and your body takes over during labour, you will instinctively know how to use your breathing to coordinate with muscle movement and ease delivery.

Dos and Don'ts

- Understand the needs of your body and if you feel any discomfort, discontinue.
- It is advisable to perform all the standing poses with your heels against the wall from the second trimester onwards.
- Avoid exercises which are performed lying on the back after the first trimester as they can reduce the blood supply to the uterus.
- Avoid *asanas* and postures that require twisting or stretching the muscles too much as they increase the risk of sprains, pulls and other

injuries. Women who were practising yoga before becoming pregnant need to be extra cautious in this regard by recognising that they should curtail the extent to which they were stretching or twisting earlier.

- Avoid any breathing exercises (*pranayama*) techniques that involve holding the breath for too long. Consult your doctor before practising *pranayama* as some techniques may not be suitable for you.

In conclusion, mild to moderate exercise is recommended in uncomplicated pregnancies. Your doctor will determine if your pregnancy is healthy enough for a controlled exercise plan or caution you against certain or any exercise if your case is complicated. Discontinue exercising if you experience pain, cramps, bleeding, dizziness, leakage, persistent headaches or persistent swelling in the ankles. Caution should not be thrown out of the window.

Embracing a healthy lifestyle in pregnancy can culminate in a generally healthy lifestyle going forward which can prove beneficial now and in the future. Continuation of a regular exercise regimen can significantly reduce risk factors associated with diabetes, obesity and high blood pressure.

Glossary

1. **Body Mass Index (BMI):** A measure that tells you the ratio of fat to muscle in your body. Body Mass Index is calculated as weight in kilograms/(height in metres)^2.

2. **Lamaze philosophy of birth:** A comprehensive approach to childbirth based on controlled breathing techniques.

3. **Hypnobirthing:** A method consisting of special breathing and relaxation techniques to induce hypnosis. The process is intended to help the expectant mother to use hypnosis as a distraction from fear and pain during delivery.

4. **Epidural injection (used in childbirth):** An injection of a pain-relieving drug into the spine in the lower back area so the mother does not feel pain during labour and delivery.

5. **Gestational diabetes:** Diabetes during pregnancy which usually reverts to normalcy after delivery.

6. **Preeclampsia:** Refers to increase in blood pressure after 20 weeks of pregnancy.

7. **Low impact aerobics:** Typically, more gentle on the body because the exercises aim to prevent joint injuries while giving one a beneficial increase in the heart rate. For pregnant women, these usually involve keeping one foot on the ground at all times without kicking or jumping.

8. **Light weight resistance:** Resistance exercises with 1 to 2 kilo weights in each hand.

9. **Pilates:** A system of exercises using special apparatus designed to improve physical strength, flexibility and posture, and enhance mental awareness.

10. **Kegel pelvic floor exercises:** Exercises to strengthen the muscles that support the bladder, uterus and rectum.

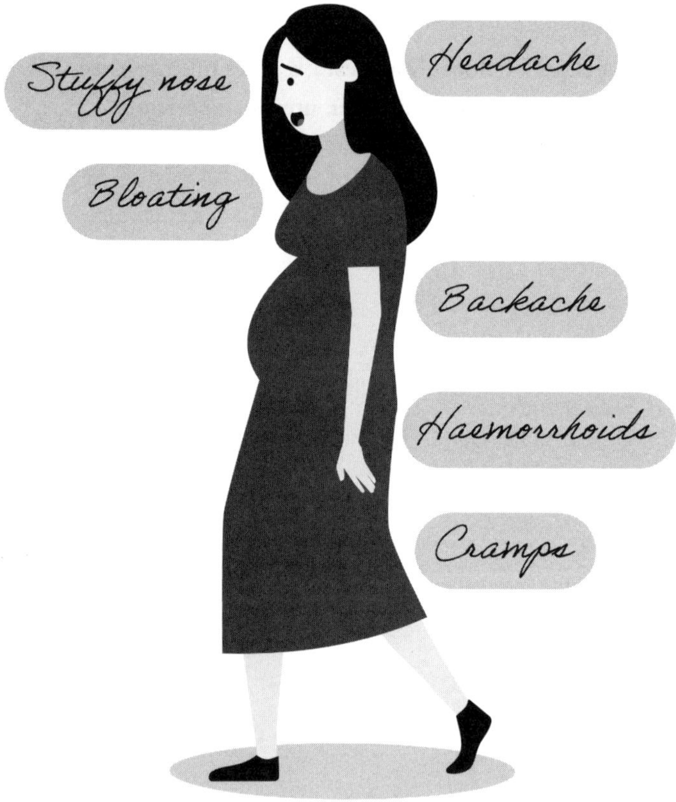
Stuffy nose
Headache
Bloating
Backache
Haemorrhoids
Cramps

CHAPTER 8

Restorative Treat Thyself Formulas

AS AN EXPECTANT MOTHER, you are likely to encounter a variety of bothersome ailments during the nine-month period. Moreover, your miseries appear to be more acute than usual. Whether they are frustrating annoyances or more specific complaints, they are normal and natural features of pregnancy. Although hard to pin down, the problem may be significant enough to make you feel very distressed. Besides, these nuisances and ailments crop up unexpectedly and you will find yourself seeking handy remedies for immediate relief and also to prevent recurring discomfort in the future.

Common complaints may manifest themselves as:

- Disorders relating to the digestive system including a bloated feeling, flatulence or gas, acidity, constipation and diarrhoea
- Headaches
- Sleeplessness and fatigue
- Breathlessness
- Bleeding Gums
- Backaches
- Varicose veins [1] and piles or haemorrhoids[2]
- Morning sickness, which can also be evening sickness for some
- Pica

The hormones of pregnancy, oestrogen and progesterone are themselves responsible for the ailments. Progesterone reduces the movement of the intestines and this makes you feel bloated and constipated. Due to the sluggishness it induces, some call it the sleepy hormone. Further, sleeplessness and fatigue go hand in hand. If you are in an office you probably feel more fatigued than sleepless.

Let us address how to deal with sleeplessness, first, as this tends to lead to fatigue. There is a scientific reason behind the old saying, "Drink a glass of warm milk before you go to sleep." Milk has tryptophan, which can induce sound sleep. Likewise, if low blood sugar levels or hypoglycemia cause sleeplessness, then a peanut butter sandwich just before going to bed can keep the blood sugar levels up. Exercise four hours before bedtime and try to have a warm bath. Have pillows in all shapes and sizes as your soulmates. Go to bed an hour earlier than you usually do, as adequate sleep reduces fatigue. If you are in the office, take short breaks to squeeze in a power nap. Additionally, if you are accustomed to yoga, breathe deeply as this can be very relaxing, but avoid deep breathing at an abnormally rapid rate.

While fatigue can ensue from sleeplessness, it is important to note that fatigue can also result from iron deficiency anaemia. If this is the case, it will be detected during your visit to the doctor who will then suggest ways to treat it.

Most of the discomfort is felt during the first three months of pregnancy, as sleeplessness and fatigue are also accompanied by nausea[3] and vomiting during that early phase. The mid phase of pregnancy is relatively relaxing although the ailments return with full force again in the last phase. What's more, you may even experience them all together.

You may be surprised to find that friends and neighbours will generally be eager to lend a helping hand in simple ways, helping with chores and doing some household errands for you. Make the most of it.

> Use home remedies to treat common problems of bloating, acidity and indigestion. Consult the doctor if they persist.

As mentioned earlier, the sleepy hormone, progesterone, induces constipation, bloated feeling, acidity, gas and indigestion. Besides this hormonal effect, reduced physical activity, improper diet and lack of adequate hydration can all lead to malfunctioning of the digestive system. Digestive ailments may also arise from an iron supplement consumed during pregnancy.

Eating a fig (*anjeer*) everyday can provide relief from constipation and also rectify anaemia. Another remedy is to eat a paste prepared by grinding a few (3 to 5) large black raisins (*munakka*) that have been previously boiled in a little water and deseeded. The consequence is to relieve one of constipation and alleviate anaemia by raising the level of haemoglobin in the blood. However, too many figs can cause tooth decay; an excess of figs (*anjeer*) and large black raisins (*munakka*) can also raise blood sugar to undesirable levels. So, stop consuming them once the constipation is dealt with. Remember to hydrate yourself well with water and other natural liquids, but not with aerated drinks or fruit juice from cartons. These latter refreshments have a high fructose content which is the culprit for gas trouble because fructose, unlike glucose, can be problematic in the intestines. When fructose is consumed in large amounts, it is not entirely digested in the small intestine. Unabsorbed fructose then gets fermented by bacteria in the large intestine producing gas. Avoid processed foods. Some natural foods, like dried fruits, honey, peanuts, vegetables like broccoli, beans, cabbage, onions and fruits such as mangoes, watermelons, apples and pears also contain high levels of fructose. So, consume these foods in quantities determined by your level of comfort. Other gas causing foods are wheat based and whole grain breakfast cereals. Well-tolerated fruits and vegetables are bananas, muskmelons and oranges, brinjals (aubergines), carrots, spinach, potatoes, radishes, corn cobs and cucumbers. In general, the absolute fructose content of food products should not be over 3 gms/serving, so portions must be sized so as not to aggravate your digestive system. Finally, wheat bran is an ideal food that passes through the digestive system without getting broken down and consequently helps in

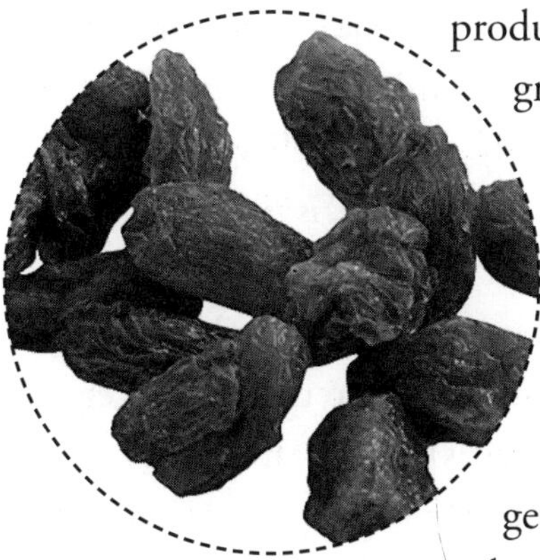

Munakka (dried raisins)

maintaining bowel regularity.

Follow the dictum: eat frequent small meals; chew thoroughly; do not talk while eating as you may swallow a lot of air; also do not drink water while eating; drink from a glass rather than a bottle or straw to avoid sucking in too much air. Avoid chewing gum; sit up while eating and drinking.

Anjeer (figs)

An enlarged uterus, water retention and consumption of high fructose containing foods, such as those mentioned earlier, can cause a feeling of being bloated. To address this, you can try some cinnamon (*dalchini*) powder with hot water and honey, like tea, or you can chew cardamom (*elaichi*) seeds. Use these remedies sparingly only to relieve bloating. A teaspoon of ginger juice and honey is another helpful alternative. Or take three or four powdered clove heads with 30cc to 40cc of warm water or chamomile tea bought off the shelf at the grocery store. Try to maintain a regular bowel habit. A useful practice is to maintain a diary where you note down the foods that don't suit you as and when you observe a pattern of digestive discomfort. Consume

Adrak (ginger)

such foods in moderate quantities or not at all. Physical exercises are recommended to relieve stress which in turn can indirectly alleviate any uneasiness due to gas. Physical exercises also increase intestinal movement, thereby preventing a feeling of being bloated.

As you may have guessed correctly, one thing leads to another. Breathlessness accompanies a feeling of being bloated and suffering from flatulence (gas). The diaphragm[4] gets pushed up and there is insufficient space for lung expansion. This can also result from the growing uterus. Avoid excess weight gain. Eat an early dinner and something light, like fruits or dalia or oats at bedtime. Remain in a propped up or inclined position for a while after a meal before lying down to sleep. Breathlessness can also be due to anaemia, a condition that your doctor can advise you about.

The most nagging discomfort of nausea and vomiting in pregnancy can be tackled by eating meals in small portions every now and then. Ginger, surprisingly, is very effective in addressing nausea in pregnancy, so grated ginger can be added to several traditionally cooked dishes, such as, *khichdi* or *pongal, kadhi* and *dal.* Of course, sipping warm ginger water (ginger boiled in water) is a good idea too. Avoid oily and spicy foods. Consult your doctor for suitable medications, if normal remedies don't provide relief.

It is generally believed that headaches are caused by excessive gas. This is partly true, in an indirect way, as gas causes sleeplessness that can induce a headache. In any case, avoid any factor that you observe to have triggered a headache, so as to prevent one in the future. Those who suffer from migraine should avoid the four Cs—Caffeine, Cheese, Chocolates and Cod (certain types of fish). Make sure to sleep enough and eat small helpings of food. Listen to soothing music, meditate and practise deep breathing to relieve headaches arising from tension.

Further, when necessary, use a cold compress, massage the head and neck and sleep in a dark room to promote sleep. You can also place chilled, used tea bags on the eyelids. Acupressure and acupuncture are other ways to try to relieve headaches. In today's lifestyle, constant work on the computer

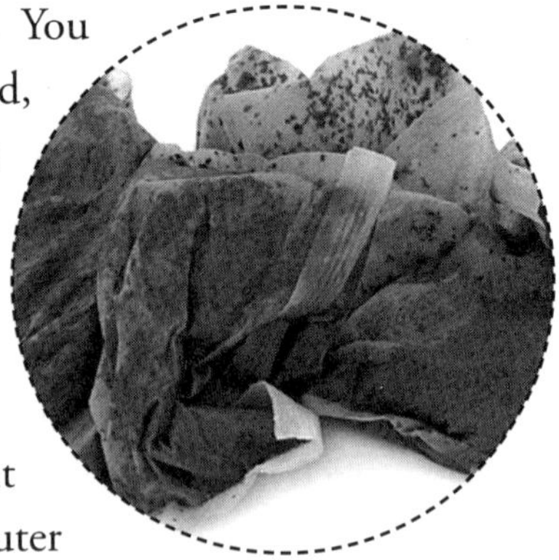

Chilled, used tea bags

must be interspersed with breaks and brief eye and neck exercises. Screen protection (on the monitor) is recommended to prevent a headache. Finally, consult your doctor if headaches persist in spite of taking all precautions.

> The second trimester is the most comfortable period of pregnancy.

Diarrhoea or passing more than three loose stools in a day is a well-known occurrence during pregnancy. The causes may be simple, such as being induced by a drug (as with an iron supplement) or due to poor food hygiene. Refrain from eating out too often. Ensure good hydration and avoid milk and milk products when experiencing diarrhoea. Consume probiotics[5] and avoid troublesome foods. If diarrhoea continues to persist, it can lead to dehydration and premature labour pains. If you feel increasingly thirsty, tired, dry in the mouth, sleepless, and notice a low output of deeply coloured or yellowish urine, then it is likely that you are dehydrated. Consult your doctor about your symptoms and take steps to treat them. In case you need it, a method to prepare an Oral rehydration solution (ORS) at home is suggested on the next page.

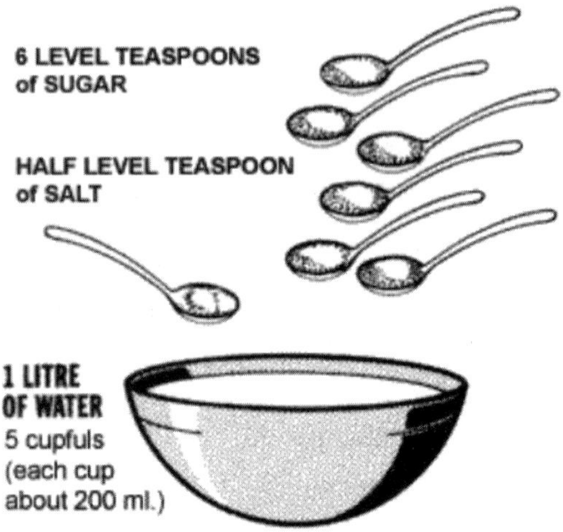

Figure 2 Home-made ORS
Source: www.rehydrate.org

Oral rehydration solution (ORS) home preparation
After washing hands and container with boiled and cooled water, stir sugar and salt into boiled and cooled water in quantities as indicated in the diagram. Do not boil the ORS once prepared. Note that ORS packets are available at no cost in government hospitals and at minimal cost elsewhere.

Bleeding gums: If, one fine morning, you spot blood on your toothbrush, it may be an indication of gum infection. Plaque (food deposition) leads to bacterial deposits and gingivitis (gingivitis gravidarum) or infection of the gums. You may also notice bad breath. To deal with this, brush often with a soft toothbrush and use dental floss to avoid getting food trapped between teeth. You may also use a mouthwash to kill odour-causing bacteria.

Again, pregnancy hormones can cause dilated blood vessels leading to varicose veins of the legs and haemorrhoids (piles). Put your feet up when seated and avoid standing for long stretches at a time, as a precautionary measure. If varicose veins have already appeared, however, consult a doctor. If they are painful and severe, you may need to wear graduated elastic stockings your doctor will prescribe for you. Similarly, the growing uterus exerts pressure on the dilated blood vessels near the anal opening[6]; the piles that are formed can sometimes even burst and bleed. Take steps to avoid constipation (as outlined earlier in this chapter) and prevent worsening of the piles. Those that have bulged out of the anal opening can cause severe pain and discomfort. Piles can be treated using local creams that are available over the counter in pharmacies. Applying pure coconut oil may be of immediate help. A Sitz Bath (hip bath) where you can sit in a tub of warm water for about 10 minutes gives immense relief.

A not-so-frequent condition in pregnancy is Pica which is an eating disorder that causes one to eat substances that have no nutritive value. Pregnant women suffering from pica usually crave chalk, mud, or stones.

The reason for this is unclear but stress is definitely considered a possible factor. Iron deficiency may be another reason. Simple solutions to deal with the problem are to chew sugarless gum, roasted *chana* or a chewable calcium tablet.

As this chapter suggests, there are some quick-fix elixirs and remedies that can be tried at home, but common sense must prevail when it's time to consult your doctor if the discomfort you are struggling with persists.

Glossary

1. **Varicose veins:** Swollen twisted veins which can cause an ache or swelling of the legs. The growing womb, progesterone hormone and increased blood flow in pregnancy are responsible for varicose veins.

2. **Haemorrhoids:** Also known as piles, haemorrhoids are swollen veins in the walls of the anus and around the rectum.

3. **Nausea:** Sick feeling with an urge to vomit.

4. **Diaphragm:** A major dome shaped muscle for respiration located below the lungs.

5. **Probiotics:** Live bacteria and yeast that promote digestion and keep the gut healthy. Traditional curd and buttermilk are examples of food sources for probiotics.

6. **Anal opening:** Outlet through which stools are eliminated from the body.

CHAPTER 9

Preoccupations that Pep You Up

ONCE THE EUPHORIA following confirmation of pregnancy has calmed down, the months ahead may feel like a rather long wait. Natural physical changes will remind you of your special situation quite often. However, they may feel inadequate as an outlet for your excitement and expectations. This is when turning your attention to maternity wear and baby essentials will come to your rescue. Set out shopping with a list in hand and a good mood, knowing you are in control after absorbing the following tips.

A relaxed stress-free approach sends positive vibes to your baby.

Maternity wear

Take a long-term view and shop for maternity wear that can adapt to different body shapes as your pregnancy progresses through various stages. Of course, you are going to choose clothes that flatter your new, glowing form. Logically, an expectant mother should select ones that are designed in a manner that they can be worn even post delivery. From this perspective, fabrics like cotton-spandex blend[1], lycra[2] and jersey knit are preferable as they are created to stretch and adjust and last for the entire length of pregnancy and beyond. Try clothes on before purchasing them to ensure that they are not itchy or sticky. Buy apparel that can be layered, so that you can peel off or add clothes to cope with fluctuating temperatures. Nursing bras or front open camisoles or shirts can prove useful in public places. Remember to wear comfortable, supportive shoes and perhaps add some scarves and jewellery to compliment your new look!

Baby essentials

Prepare to welcome your baby with super soft clothing. One piece pyjamas and full-sleeved garments made of cotton are ideal for summers. For winters, fleece[3] is generally practical. Gather some socks or booties and caps to coordinate with the outfits. And don't forget to keep mittens handy to cover the little nails in order to protect the baby's face and body from being scratched.

Baby powders have little to offer other than fragrance. For this and other reasons, it is best to avoid them altogether. Baby powder is often touted as a way to prevent prickly heat, but, in actual usage, it tends to accumulate in the folds of the skin and cause irritation. If applied on the face, there is a danger of the baby inhaling small or fine particles present in talc. Other types of baby powders such as those

> *Choose maternity apparel that can be layered, in stretchy non-itchy fabrics.*

containing corn starch can aggravate any existing yeast infection and cause nappy rash. Gentle soaps, like Syndet soaps and those with natural ingredients like aloe vera, mild shampoos and moisturisers may be a part of the shopping list. Towels, preferably with a hood to keep baby warm are essential as babies lose body warmth quickly after a bath.

> Avoid hand-me-down toys from the 60s or 70s due to lead in the paint.

Finally, the most desired items on the list, namely, toys for the newborn, must be bought after careful consideration, taking into account the manufacturer's warning if any. Choose light, unbreakable and colourful toys with smooth edges sans ribbons, lace or beaded necklaces, as babies can get accidentally entangled and strangled in them. Washable, stuffed, soft and cuddly toys without buttons and baubles[4] are considered most appropriate at this stage. Hand-me-down toys as old as from the 60s and 70s are likely to be decorated with paint containing lead and are best avoided. If thinking of buying a toy chest, plan for the long term and get one with holes for ventilation.

Assuming you have advanced to the seventh month,

sit back and prepare for the heart-warming "*Godh Bharai*" ceremony, also called a Baby Shower. Incredibly, this ritual, known by a variety of names, is practised in several regions of the world and in different parts of our country in one form or the other. Family members and friends consider mother and baby to have entered a safe phase of pregnancy. So, everyone is ready to celebrate motherhood and shower blessings on the yet-to-be-born baby. In India, the custom, generally, is to schedule the ritual in an odd month for luck, hence the popularity of the seventh month, although celebrations are not unknown as late as the ninth month. *Poojas* are performed and the mother-to-be is blessed with garlands and bangles. According to current trends, baby showers may include favours and themes, which may require some advance planning. Occasionally, a mother-to-be may wish to host one herself. If you are one of those women who like to organise a celebration for themselves, consider hiring an event planner or reaching out to a helpful friend. While the shopping list may seem endless, it can be thrilling to shop for gifts, eatables and decorations.

The nine-month-long wait can be a joyful ride for the father-to-be too. The vitalising feeling of elation will be complete if he is by your side helping and participating in everything you do, whether it is shopping or attending antenatal classes with you.

This is the perfect occasion for you to occupy centre stage while family and friends are fussing over you!

Glossary

1. **Cotton-spandex blend:** Pure cotton does not stretch, so it is blended with a small percentage of a stretchy yarn called spandex or elastane in the spinning process to add stretch to the fabric.

2. **Lycra:** A synthetic fabric valued for its elasticity. Lycra is widely used in sports clothes, denims and blended into fabrics where elasticity is desired. Elastane and spandex are similar products.

3. **Fleece:** A kind of fabric woven with a deep nap or pile which feels soft and warm to the touch, like wool. Most popularly used fleece is made from polyester although some varieties incorporate natural fibres like cotton and wool.

4. **Bauble:** A small showy ornament that is usually spherical and brightly coloured.

CHAPTER 10

Bringing Baby Home: Notes for the Family

PREPARING FOR A new arrival must be carefully considered not only by the Mother but also by the Father and the Sibling/s-to-be, if any. This practice is of utmost importance and should not be ignored.

Notes addressing mom

Both you and your partner will experience incredible excitement when you become aware of your pregnancy. However, these feelings may slowly give way to anxiety. Every 'Papa-to-be' reacts differently and so does a sibling, especially if it is the first time a new arrival is expected. You and your partner may have planned to have a baby together, but this does not preclude either of you from experiencing conflicting emotions when faced with the reality of the situation. So, lay the groundwork together to approach parenthood as a positive challenge. Although the needs of the newly growing baby will compete with commitments you have to your husband, you can work through this together as a couple with adequate understanding and organisation.

Notes addressing dad

As a father-to-be for the first time, you will understand your role and learn how to face each new situation naturally, as is the case with an expectant mother. Your part is very critical to the quality of your partner's pregnancy and health of the baby. For example, if you smoke, use drugs or consume alcohol, it is equally important for you to avoid these habits, as it is for your pregnant partner to make a similar lifestyle change. As a father, you can start by accompanying your partner for every antenatal checkup and following what the doctor has to say. You must recognise and understand the emotional changes that pregnancy hormones cause in the mother. For example, nausea and vomiting in pregnancy may inhibit her from savouring a meal outside the home. Likewise, she may exhibit a temporary lack of sexual interest, partly due to fear that the baby may be hurt. There is no need to be anxious that the baby may be harmed as it is well cushioned and protected by the fluid around it. Remember that this is a passing phase and these changes should not let frustration, depression and resentment set in. Discuss your concerns with thoughtful friends, who are fathers themselves.

The first-time father can attend childbirth classes and practise necessary skills, such as how to hold the baby, change diapers, and also feed, burp and get the baby to sleep. In addition to this training, Dad can plan for financial obligations and check on the possibility of taking paternity leave.

Notes to the couple

You may be concerned about your sexual life, and the way in which it can be affected. As mentioned in the 'Notes addressing dad', an expectant mother may be hesitant to have sex. Although sex is a normal part of pregnancy, some women experience a temporary lack of sexual desire. Usually, this happens in the first trimester. Libido improves in the second trimester. In the third trimester, sex may stimulate uterine contractions, so one has to be cautious. Find alternative ways to restore and maintain intimacy. Candlelight dinners can be organised and indulged in at home. Even if sex is not desired, intimacy can still be sustained through kissing and cuddling; perhaps also by talking and singing to your baby, together.

> Fathers, please accept your pregnant wife's temporary lack of sexual interest.

While waiting for the approaching due date, you can plan and prepare the room for your baby's arrival together. Safety must be a top priority. Prevent direct drafts of breeze from affecting the newborn by placing the cradle away from the window or the air conditioner vent. Consider soft colours for walls so that they are pleasing to the eye and soothing to the baby. There are many ways to decorate and express your feelings for your baby. They include providing soft, stuffed toys, putting up cartoon figures on the walls, or selecting baby furniture, clothes, booties and toiletries. Step back and feel proud about the room both of you have specially designed for your baby.

Keep hospital records ready and make sure all necessary phone numbers are handy. It is a good idea to note down phone numbers for ambulance services in case of an emergency. Last but not least, check with the hospital's customer care personnel about the policy on payment methods and remember to take necessary funds with you, as cash, credit card or cheque based on what the hospital accepts.

As the time for delivery draws near, make sure that a maternity bag is ready. Discuss how to manage pain when the need arises and be alert for any warning signs that may mean an immediate visit to the hospital.

Notes to care for the sibling-to-be

If you are parents of one or more children already, then pay attention to preparing each sibling-to-be for the changes ahead. Involve them in everything you do to bring home the new baby. If the sibling-to-be is old enough, get him/her to gently touch pregnant Mom's belly, sing and feel the baby's movements. Take him/her to visit relatives and friends who have babies and encourage interaction with them. Let him/her accompany you to the hospital to witness your antenatal checkups and hear the baby's heartbeat.

The completely secure world your child has become accustomed to until this new turn of events, may begin to feel less certain. So, take extra care to make the existing child feel just as important and equally valued as the expected baby.

Overall, you and your partner must both be aware that emotional and physical adjustments will have to be made. Be as open as possible when you discuss these matters and use stress-free strategies to cruise through the nine months of pregnancy.

Checklist for items to be packed in the maternity bag

- Comfortable, loose, front-open clothing
- Hot water bottle
- Maternity/nursing bras
- Towel
- Toiletries
- Maternity pads
- Baby-booties and mittens
- Soft muslin cloth
- Baby blanket
- Nappies
- Case file
- Insurance papers
- Hand sanitizers
- Antiseptic cleaning wipes

Recognition of labour and delivery

When you are close to the due date the doctor will explain the kinds of red flag signs that you should be alert to, as they may require you to report to the hospital immediately. Advice about such indicators is usually given when you are around 36 weeks into the pregnancy.

In chapter 3, I described the amniotic fluid as the protective medium in which the foetus is developing into a baby. Both the fluid and foetus, as you may be aware, are contained in a sac or bag (referred to as a water bag) inside the womb or uterus. If it feels like some pains have begun or the water bag has burst and you notice what is known as "leaking", then it is a sure signal that you should report to the hospital. You should also head there if you observe decreased foetal movements or notice a thick discharge, referred to as "show", from the vagina.

Towards the latter part of pregnancy you might feel your uterus tightening on and off, yet not associated with pain. Gradually this feeling of recurring, periodic tightening, known as Braxton Hicks contractions[1], does become linked with pain and progresses into full-fledged labour pains. If you recall what period pains feel like, you are likely to easily recognise labour pains as they are basically a very severe form of period pains. As labour pains progress, they slowly increase in intensity and frequency.

In a normal pregnancy, the water bag ruptures when the woman is in advanced labour. But in a small percentage of women, it can burst even when labour has not begun. Sometimes, as you approach the date of delivery you may notice your clothes getting wet without warning, leading you to

> *Ensure that siblings continue to feel secure. Involve them in everything you do to prepare them to welcome the baby with a positive attitude.*

presume that you have lost your capacity to control your urine. However, if you notice that the smell of the wet undergarment is not that of urine but something else, then, your water bag has probably ruptured. This is when you are "leaking" and is one of those signs that you should go to the hospital. It is prudent to wear white undergarments so that the colour of the leaking fluid can be noted.

The first time a pregnant woman feels the baby move (known as quickening) can occur between 20 and 22 weeks. It is extremely important that she pays careful attention to these movements or kicks. Such awareness becomes even more important as the pregnancy advances into the last few weeks. The significance of this aspect cannot be stressed more than by reminding you that the expecting mother is the only one who can keep track of foetal movements. Your doctor will tell you how to keep count of baby's kicks! Generally, you are expected to feel at least 1 to 2 foetal movements every hour.

Alternatively, if you rest on your left side after a meal, then you should feel at least 10 movements over a 2 hour period. If no kicks are felt in three to four consecutive hours, then you should report to the hospital. By convention, if there are no movements for 12 consecutive hours then it is a very serious sign. The answer to question 13 in the FAQs section at the end of the book sheds more light on counting and understanding baby's kicks. This will help you recognise what is called a "movement alarm signal" or MAS and decide on the urgency of heading to the hospital immediately.

A thick plug of mucus is discharged when the mouth of the uterus (called cervix) begins to open. The discharge, called "show" may or may not be blood-stained. Again, as there is evidence that the cervix is opening, it is time to head to the hospital.

If you are experiencing a low-risk pregnancy, your doctor will just let you wait until you get spontaneous pains. If you have already crossed the due date then the doctor may consider inducing labour pain using medication. The course of action that a doctor will take can only be determined on an individualised, case by case basis, involving many medical factors.

A word on caesarean section

Most pregnant women are aware that a baby is delivered as intended by nature but have also heard talk of the baby being removed surgically from the womb.

Naturally, a pregnant woman is likely to be curious or concerned about whether she will have a normal delivery or by surgical procedure, also known as a caesarean section (C-section). In this procedure, the lower part of the abdomen is cut to deliver the baby, the abdomen being the part of the human body below the chest containing the stomach, intestines and reproductive organs. In common parlance, we refer to it as the belly. Most of the time a C-section is done under regional anaesthesia although general anaesthesia may be administered when necessary under certain conditions. Before the procedure, a tube called a catheter is inserted into the bladder to allow urine to drain into a bag, which is removed after 15 to 18 hours. This is what is meant when the doctor says that the bladder will be catheterised. If within 24 hours of delivery you are able to walk without any problem and you have started consuming liquids followed by food, then you can go home in 48 to 72 hours after the procedure.

Although your labour pains may be progressing smoothly, emergencies can arise unexpectedly. There could be an abrupt shift in the rate of the baby's heartbeat, either dropping suddenly or rising to a very high level. At other times, an emergency may be indicated by the amniotic fluid looking thick and greenish—referred to as being stained by "meconium" (see the FAQs for more details). Or the progress of labour may fail because the bony passage may be inadequate for the baby to pass through. In such situations, you will probably be told that the baby will be delivered by a "caesarean section" procedure.

A C-section becomes necessary in circumstances where the life of the mother or baby or both lives have to be saved. However, there are not many situations during the course of the pregnancy in which the need for the operation can be predicted definitively. Even when it is very likely that a C-section will have to be done the doctor decides on the procedure only a few weeks before delivery. One kind of predicament arises when the placenta[2] completely covers the mouth of the uterus, also called the cervical os, leaving no space for the baby to come out normally.

This condition can actually be life threatening if the couple does not elect to proceed with the operation before the onset of labour pains, as severe bleeding may ensue once the pains begin. Another reason to expect a C-section may have to do with the position of the baby. Normally, the baby appears head first during delivery. But abnormal positions of the baby in the uterus, especially those that do not meet the criteria for manual rectification by the doctor, will require delivery by C-section.

At other times, very high, uncontrolled blood pressure or uncontrolled blood sugar, or other medical conditions that the mother is suffering from, may be why a C-section is advised. An often noted condition among Indians is called Obstetric cholestasis of pregnancy[3] which requires the baby to be delivered once mature, which is at 37 weeks. However, the uterus is not yet ready to respond to induced labour at this stage since changes in the uterus, in preparation for delivery, begin to happen only in the last 2 to 3 weeks. So, if an attempt is made to induce labour early as a consequence of Obstetric cholestasis, it is uncertain if labour will commence and a C-section may be the only option.

> Sometimes a caesarean section becomes necessary for safeguarding yours and the baby's life, so don't be afraid.

A C-section will also be considered if the baby's growth is very poor and it is determined that the baby will not be able to withstand the stress of labour. Tests, such as, a "Doppler ultrasound"[4] and a "Cardiotocograph (CTG)" may be used to predict foetal well being. A CTG is a recording of foetal heart sounds on a graph while the mother simultaneously intimates foetal movements by pressing a button. The doctor will interpret the graph and act accordingly. If the graph is not normal, the doctor will opt for a C-section.

As I have already stated, there are only a few indications, such as those described above that allow a C-section to be decided upon with certainty, in the weeks before delivery. Often, C-sections are done when emergencies arise during active labour that are alarming enough to need urgent action.

Occasionally, patients voluntarily opt for a C-section, perhaps due to fear of labour pains. While counselling, the doctor will describe various methods used to help patients cope with labour pains. In one popular method, medicine is injected into a space in the spinal cord, called the epidural space, allowing the patient to not feel pain even during the progress of labour. This is the method being considered when "epidural analgesia" is mentioned. If the patient insists on surgery in spite of counselling, then it is a case of "cesarean delivery on maternal request" or CDMR. Indeed, some patients desire to deliver the baby at an auspicious time and there are those couples who believe that a lax vagina following normal delivery may reduce pleasure in sexual life later and prefer to opt for a C-section procedure.

There is a lot of hue and cry these days about doctors doing unnecessary C-sections. Note, however, that the doctor usually counsels the patient and her family before the operation and takes an informed consent. Whenever feasible, the family should feel free to clarify all their doubts before consenting and take a second opinion, if not satisfied, instead of presuming it was unnecessary.

Glossary

1. **Braxton Hicks contractions:** Spontaneous, infrequent, painless tightening of the uterus usually noticed in the third trimester.

2. **Placenta:** A flattened circular organ that is filled with blood vessels. It is attached to the uterus on one side and provides nutrients and oxygen to the baby through the umbilical cord, which is attached to its inner surface.

3. **Obstetric cholestasis of pregnancy:** Cholestasis is a situation when the liver cannot excrete bile properly and manifests as severe itching all over the body especially on the hands and feet. If it happens during pregnancy it is called Obstetric cholestasis of pregnancy.

4. **Doppler ultrasound:** An imaging procedure to detect blood flow in the uterus, placenta and baby.

CHAPTER 11

The Awakening: A New Chapter Begins!

The postnatal phase

CELEBRATIONS ARE FOLLOWED by a reality check after going home, an environment sans nurses and hospital staff to turn to for help. You begin to realise that looking after a baby is a round-the-clock job. In fact, you need to take care of yourself and the baby at the same time, and yet remain physically and mentally healthy. Besides, you also want to cherish motherhood in spite of noticing a bit of unintentional neglect by the family. The focus has shifted to the baby and the family members sometimes fail to realise that the mother, who has just delivered the baby, also needs attention and care.

Glowing new mother.

The postnatal phase is akin to a teething problem for you and is just as new to your baby too. Nappy changing is a challenge for you initially while breastfeeding is a new essential skill to be mastered by both you and your baby. You need not feel guilty if you find that your maternal instincts are not up to the mark, because in due course, you will gain more confidence as you regain your strength, find solutions to your struggles and take up the demands of motherhood.

The confinement period of the first six weeks after delivery is very important, irrespective of whether it was a vaginal delivery or Caesarean section (C-section). Inevitably, there will be some pain in the stitch area following either kind of delivery. Of course, you can talk to your doctor about taking a suitable painkiller if you want one. After a vaginal (normal) delivery, you may sense occasional inability to control (also known as incontinence) urine and gas. Kegel exercises[1] can help you recuperate from any such embarrassing episodes. Although the external wound in a C-section appears to have healed, the invisible internal wound is still raw. As with any wound, the internal area of the C-section wound takes a full six-week-period to heal properly. So plan to rest during this phase to allow the body to recover completely and focus your attention on your newborn as this is the best time to discover the special bond between you and your baby.

Dehydration can result from trying to shrink or control the distended abdomen by drinking only small quantities of water (see para on diarrhoea in chapter 8 for how to recognise if you are dehydrated). Sometimes advice of this nature is given by well-meaning elderly relatives and friends, based on traditional methods practised by older generations. Whatever you do to get back in shape make sure to strike the right balance in water intake to remain adequately hydrated. Likewise, water boiled with carom seeds (*ajwain*) or cumin seeds (*jeera*) is often offered constantly to encourage lactation. As it is served very hot, women merely sip it and find it difficult to drink enough to satisfy the body's needs. If it is not to your liking, then ask for some boiled *ajwain* water cooled to room temperature or plain cool water, when you desire a change.

'Postpartum blues' is a term used for a temporary 'low feeling' which can be overcome with your personal effort and help from near and dear ones. Here are some tips to help you:

- Sleep when your baby sleeps instead of treating it as an opportunity to perform other chores before the baby wakes up again. Don't be surprised to find that you are falling asleep despite the odd hours, possibly due to sheer fatigue. You will feel less exhausted by resting and consequently enjoy everything that you do.
- Feeding the baby is entirely your job, but it is helpful if someone else can take up baby's burping, or else by the time you burp your baby you will find it is nearly time for the next feed!

Nightie designed for feeding.

Continue having a balanced diet and follow the good hydration regimen that you practised during pregnancy. Be aware that crash diets decrease milk production. Limit caffeine intake and increase intake of liquids such as water, milk and

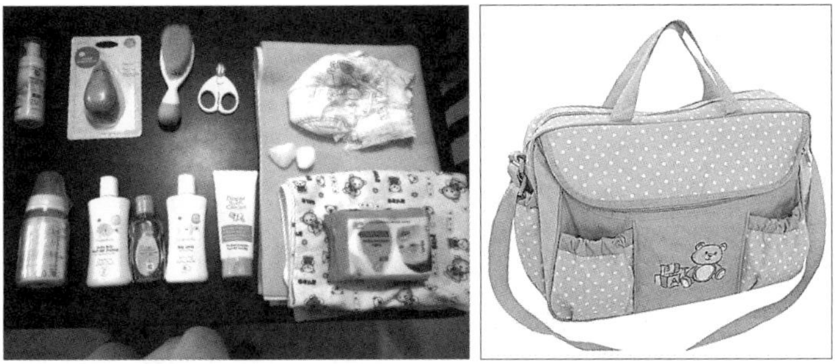

Kit for baby.

fresh juices. What does not suit you will not suit your baby too. As infants depend on mother's milk, you should have a diet which includes different foods that are rich in all nutrients so that the flavours are relished by your baby also.

Nature's gift, breast milk is the best milk. Breast milk has all the nutrients that the baby needs for his/her growth and development. Antibodies present in breast milk build up the baby's immunity against a variety of viruses and bacteria including protecting the baby from ailments such as diarrhoea and ear infections. The risk of suffering from asthma and allergies is reduced in a baby who is breastfed for at least six months.

Some painful conditions, such as cracked nipples, can be tackled by applying doctor-recommended creams between feeds, until the soreness heals. You can continue to breastfeed using a nipple shield[2]. Alternatively, you can spoon feed or use a paladai[3], after expressing milk.

An important precaution to take here is to thoroughly wash and dry the nipple shield and paladai before use. In particular, take care to ensure that there is no residual,

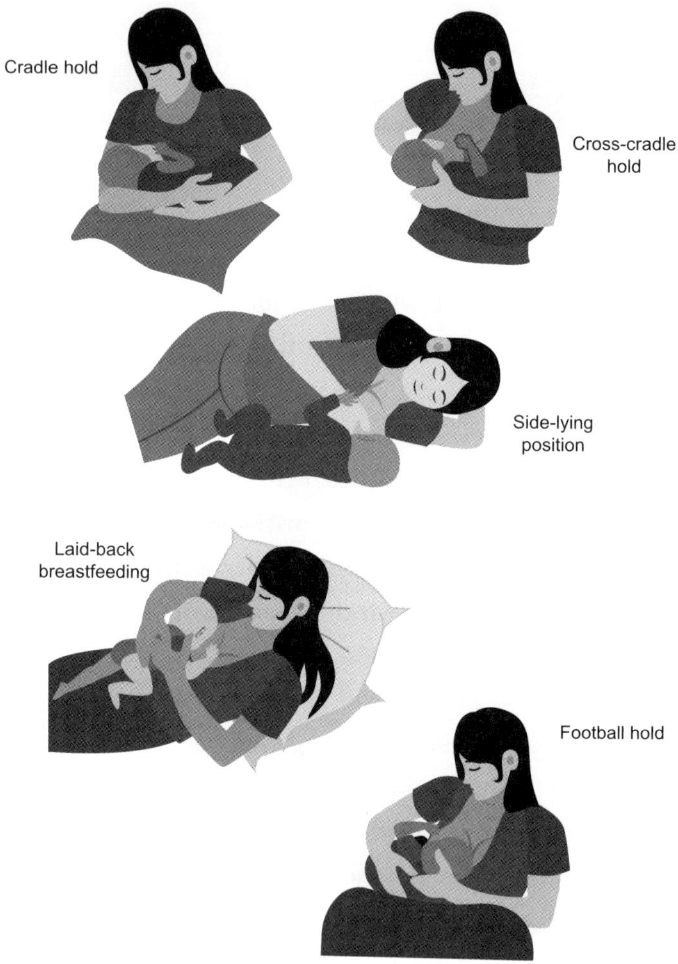

Figure 3 Breast-feeding positions.

curdled breast milk from an earlier feed left in the ridges of the nipple shield. Formula feeds need not be resorted to since you can use the nipple shield while sore and discard it once the pain disappears. Retracted nipples can be gently massaged outward with creams, starting ideally from the antenatal period to avoid their development in the first place. Night feeds can be stressful, but this is a temporary phase. As the sucking reflexes of the baby strengthen and your milk increases, more milk is consumed and a satisfied baby lets you sleep longer.

Formula milk is sweeter than breast milk and, if given too often, the baby will gradually reject your milk. Avoid bottle feeding even if it is your own milk being fed. Bottle feeding leads to nipple confusion and creates subsequent problems for the baby when he or she needs to latch on to the breast. In some situations, nevertheless, bottle feeding may become necessary as there may be a medical contraindication[4] to breastfeeding. The doctor will inform you about it, if it applies to you. If you are experiencing a fever, it is not a contraindication to breastfeed unless the fever persists, but be sure to consult your doctor if it does not subside. In case you have a fever, use a face mask when you feed the baby. Never allow the breast to get engorged[5] as it can lead to 'milk fever', pain and chills. You can express the engorged breasts after hot-water fomentation and the milk will flow out with comparative ease.

In India, many natural beverages and foods are believed to increase lactation and promote recuperation. Traditional drinks prepared by boiling carom seeds (*ajwain*), sacred basil (*tulsi*), fennel seeds (*saunf*) or cumin seeds (*jeera*) in water, may be consumed like tea. Other suggested beverages are almond (*badam*) milk and turmeric in hot milk. The latter has anti-inflammatory[6] properties and is also rich in vitamin B6, vitamin C and minerals.

Among wholesome solid food options are recipes with dry ginger (*saunth chutney*), mung beans (*moong*) and red lentils (*masoor*) for easy digestion and also the popular south Indian dish, finger millet dosa (*ragi dosa*). Traditional sweets such as *panjiri*, *gondh ke ladoo*, *halwa*, and others are recipes that combine dry fruits with ghee to induce more milk production and to help regain strength. While there is no modern scientific evidence to support these practices, consuming more calories will certainly provide more strength at this time. However, exercise caution and consume calories in moderation to lose excess weight more easily in the long run. This can be a challenge while continuing to please all the

Postpartum blues and feeling gloomy are normal and natural after baby is home.

well-meaning relatives and observing various traditions aimed at restoring your energy. You can always comply to satisfy your needs while also setting some boundaries and exercising self-restraint.

> When you look in the mirror, choose exercise over a crash diet to restore your image.

Please do not panic when you see your reflection in the mirror and rush into a crash diet. Aim for slow and steady weight loss. You must begin with simple exercises for the back and to strengthen your muscles. Although you spend time predominantly on taking care of the baby, using this as an explanation for lacking time to exercise cannot be an acceptable excuse. A good way to warm up to exercise is to take your baby out in the stroller, six weeks after delivery. While pushing the stroller, you can jog slowly in a park or around your apartment complex. You will be surprised to see your baby beaming and appreciating every moment. Thus along with your exercise this will feel like another positive accomplishment and give you something to look forward to more regularly.

Resuming a normal sexual life may cause concern for you and your partner, as you are afraid that it might be painful. Another reason can be stress, which seems to be taking a toll on you and your partner. At this point, I urge you to refer to alternative ways to maintain intimacy, mentioned under 'notes for the family', in chapter 9. Aim to have a better understanding with your partner, who may be feeling a little neglected because of the divided attention. As for the rest, life will get back to normal soon.

The surgical cut made near the vaginal opening (episiotomy) to aid in normal delivery or a scar from a caesarean section should normally take six weeks to heal. So, assuming you are mentally prepared, it is reasonable to wait until you have recovered over this time, before you resume sexual activity. However, use some form of contraception, since your body is now ready for another pregnancy.

You will not regret the six weeks of confinement because it will give you an opportunity to get back to form and feel good again. During these six weeks try not to go out even if you feel fit enough, because your immunity is still weak. You can catch infections easily, especially if you visit crowded places like malls, cinema halls or restaurants. Observe food hygiene. Even while at home, stay away from any sick member in the family and make sure people wash their hands or use sanitizer before handling your baby. For now, relax and focus on your bundle of joy.

Glossary

1. **Kegel exercises:** Simple exercises that strengthen muscles which support the uterus, bladder and rectum, which in turn provide relief from urinary incontinence and gas.

2. **Nipple shield:** A small protective shield, made of soft silicone, worn over the nipple while breastfeeding. It is designed to allow milk to flow through small holes while the baby latches on to the breast and sucks naturally.

3. **Paladai:** A small, shallow cup with a spout specially designed to feed infants, traditionally used in India. Use of the paladai is considered hygienic as it is very easy to wash and keep clean. .

4. **Contraindication:** The word used to indicate that a particular treatment is inadvisable given the observed symptoms and conditions.

5. **Engorged (breast):** When breasts become hard, swollen and painful from too much milk in them they are described as being engorged. This can result from blockages that prevent free flow of milk or because the infant is not latching on to the breast properly enough to draw all the milk out without leaving some accumulating behind.

6. **Anti-inflammatory:** Inflammation is pain, redness or swelling resulting from reaction to infection in a part of your body. An anti-inflammatory is a medicine or food stuff that has properties to reduce inflammation.

CHAPTER 12

Newborn Care: Basic Principles

NOW YOU HAVE a bundle of joy in your arms, or perhaps the baby is in the arms of a bundle of nerves? You may realise that it's one thing to read about infant care in books and quite another to be in the thick of a real-life situation. Understandably, it is time for a reality check. Take a deep breath; your inborn maternal instincts will surface and gradually evolve. But you want to know how to tackle simple tasks involved in the immediate care of your newborn, don't you?

You instinctively realise that you need to clean, feed and lull the infant to sleep to instill security in him or her. Simultaneously, you also want to strengthen the bond between the two of you. It is a learning process for both mother and baby, although you might have more to learn than your baby does! The senses, already imbibed in the womb, now help the baby recognise his or her mother, especially her voice, and this provides a feeling of security.

Begin by planning the ways in which to incorporate your essential daily chores into a schedule, carefully designating time for feeding and putting your baby to sleep. In fact, you may initially have to adjust your program around the infant's demands until both of you settle into a pattern. It is practical to sleep when your baby sleeps, particularly if you are sleepy after having woken up to feed the baby at night. Assuming there are others to lend a helping hand, consider chalking out a plan to delegate tasks that they can do. Ensure that someone will help you at night, if the need arises. Trying to play the role of Supermom is inadvisable.

Cleaning and caring for baby

Gently wipe any sticky discharge from the baby's eyes using cotton balls moistened with lukewarm, sterile water. Any persistent discharge, however, must be brought to the attention of your doctor. You will notice that your baby's nails grow very fast, which is normal, and have to be clipped using a baby nail clipper. It is best to clip

> Fathers, enjoy playing and helping with your baby, it's the best way to bond with him or her.

the nails when they are soft, which is immediately after you have bathed and put your baby to sleep.

Bathe your baby using lukewarm water and mild soap, such as Syndet, which is a skin friendly, gentle soap whose pH is similar to that of a baby's skin. It is helpful to keep necessary items such as soap, towel, and baby shampoo, among other things, within arm's reach. This enables the mother to hold the baby at all times.

Pediatricians generally recommend waiting for at least two weeks before starting to massage the baby. This waiting period is intended to allow the infant's skin barrier to develop and make it less prone to infection.

Massaging improves blood circulation and stimulates the various systems of the body such as the musculoskeletal system[1] and the nervous system. Massage is a wonderful way to communicate with your baby, especially if you are talking, or singing to him or her at the same time. A massage is relaxing and helps your baby to fall asleep. If you find your baby turning away or crying, take note of it and massage only when your baby is ready for it.

You can massage your baby either before or after a

bath. If you intend to use oil, then do it before the bath so that any greasy residue is washed away. This is especially relevant for summer months when oil that blocks the pores can cause discomfort to the baby, as it would to an adult. If you are massaging the baby after a bath, then apply appropriate moisturisers. Pure, cold pressed oils such as olive and almond oils are most suitable for a massage before the bath. Coconut oil is a good emollient, but commercial mustard oil is best avoided because it is usually adulterated. Olive oil may be used as a moisturiser even after a bath. Ensure that whichever oil is used, it is perfume-free and leaves the baby's skin non-sticky. Use a very small quantity of oil as this is sufficient for the purpose.

Dress your baby in soft cotton clothes during the summer season. When using a diaper or cotton nappy, make sure the umbilical cord is not covered as it can get soiled. It is very important to take care of the umbilical cord until it falls off, which is usually within a week to 10 days after birth. Wash your hands before you handle the cord. Clean around the base of the cord with a cotton swab dipped in sterile water. If the cord has a blood stained discharge or is emitting a foul smell and is very soft, report the observation to your doctor. More importantly, if your baby is lethargic or feverish, it can be a sign of sepsis[2] or an infection.

Diaper rash is another source of distress for the baby. This usually happens due to moisture from a wet diaper, combined with chemical irritants and infectious organisms present in the urine and faeces. Another source of rash can be due to friction caused by the wet nappy rubbing against the skin. Therefore, keep the bottom aired once in a while by placing your baby on a waterproof sheet. When the baby is wearing a diaper change it as soon as possible after it gets wet. As such

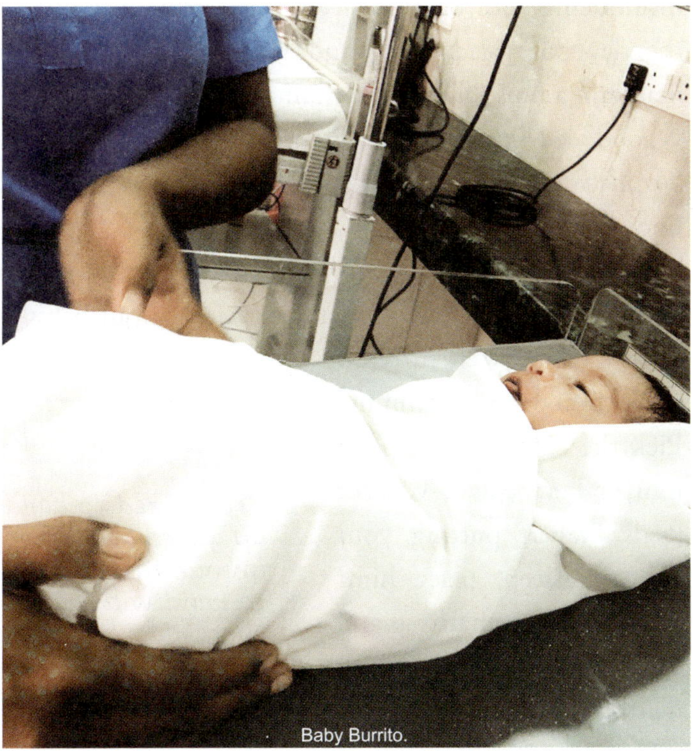

Baby Burrito.

change the diaper every 2 to 3 hours even if it is not soiled by urine and of course, change immediately if it is unclean due to faecal matter.

In what is called the Baby Burrito method, a baby is wrapped snugly around as in the image on the previous page.

The cocooning effect of this method has the potential to recreate the warmth and environment similar to that recently enjoyed in the womb. Combine this comforting feeling with a lullaby as it may be your best bet to succeed in inducing your baby to sleep. Keep baby busy during the day but tread softly and keep visitors at bay to maintain a noise-free room around a baby ready to sleep. A good feed, cosy bed, dim light, and a quiet atmosphere are all conducive to helping your baby have a long and undisturbed sleep.

You may feel like having your baby next to you when you sleep, but it is recommended that you put baby in a baby cot adjacent to your bed from the beginning. Pick the baby up and place him or her next to you for feeds. When putting your baby to sleep, place him/her on a firm mattress and on his/her back. Avoid plush mattresses, sofas, or sofa

Breast feed to build up your baby's immunity and also to bond with your child.

cushions. Make sure there are no stuffed toys in the crib or around the baby. Try not to overbundle the infant while the fan is switched off, so that the baby falls asleep in a comfortable temperature. All these precautions help to allay any fear of Sudden Infant Death Syndrome[3] (SIDS) also known as cot death. If you are very tired or have taken some sleep inducing medication, such as cough syrup, resist the urge to sleep right next to your baby so as not to accidentally roll over him or her.

As with adults, an important aspect of care is to protect your baby from being bitten by mosquitoes. Ensure that the baby is covered in clothing with full sleeves and full pants, preferably in light shades. Keep the surroundings clean and have a fan on to allow for movement of air. Use a mosquito net or electronic mosquito repellent device and be sure to take baby out at times when there are fewer mosquitoes around.

Prepare to feed your baby on a demand basis which can be expected once every two hours in the first two months. Babies tend to sleep for much of the 24-hour daily cycle. So, in practice, try to maintain a semi-demand schedule by waking up the sleeping baby and feeding him or her if the two-hour interval has ended. If you notice your baby's head turning towards anything that strokes the cheek or mouth, also called 'rooting', or you hear sucking sounds or your baby snuggles to your breast, then this is an indication that

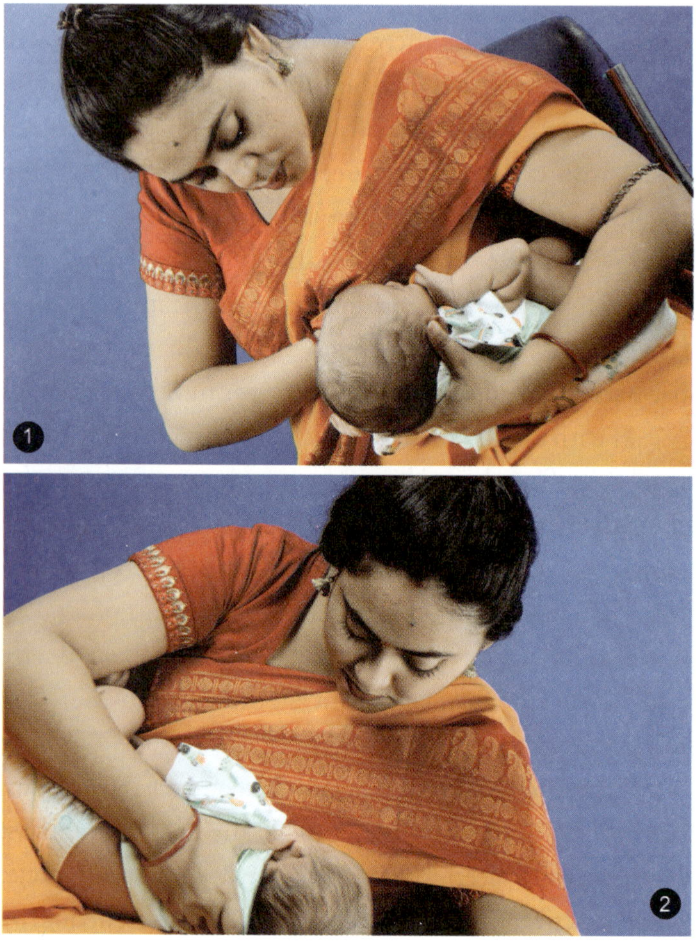

BREAST-FEEDING POSITIONS: 1 Football hold useful for those who had a C.section or have large breasts 2 cross-cradle hold.

he/she is hungry and ready to be fed. It is best to feed the baby as soon as you observe these signs, rather than delay until the baby cries in spite of being comforted. Maintain

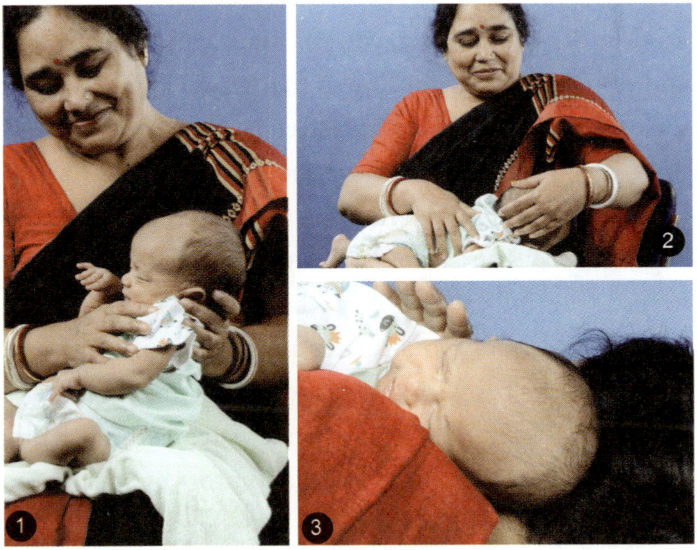

BURPING POSITIONS: 1 Hold your baby sitting up on your lap across your knee 2 Lay your baby on your lap on his or her belly. 3 Sit upright and hold your baby against your chest, keeping baby's chin resting on your shoulder.

a good daily diet while breastfeeding, drinking up to 2.5 litres of fluid, including 2 to 3 glasses of milk, for good lactation. Consuming a glass of fluid just before a feed is believed to be especially effective. Any enhancement in milk production is really dependent on how well the baby sucks the breast.

In the initial stages, difficulties with breastfeeding may be a source of concern but bear in mind that sucking is the best reflex for increasing milk output. Proper flow should usually get established by the third day. For the first two months, feeds are usually on demand. After six months of age, however, you can train your baby to feed and rest in a regular routine so that you are able to get at least four hours of sleep at a stretch. If necessary, breast milk can be stored for short spells of upto 4 hours in the summer and upto 6 hours in cooler temperatures (30 degrees Celsius and below). This also allows someone else to feed your milk to the baby while you rest. Discard any leftover milk, and avoid the temptation to store or freeze it. Hold your baby in a comfortable position creating a 'nursing nest'[4] while you breastfeed. After feeding, gently help baby relieve bloating and discomfort by burping to let the air out. Breastfed babies may develop diarrhoea. Consult the doctor if that happens to your baby. You may be instructed to feed the baby an oral rehydration solution if the diarrhoea is severe (refer to chapter 8 for details about preparing the ORS if you want to prepare it at home).

Bonding with dad

'Engrossment' describes the process of close and mutual bonding between a father and his baby. This can begin early, for example, by talking to the baby even while he/she is in the womb. The parents-to-be can plan and prepare for the big day together to bring baby home. In general, fathers are not allowed in delivery rooms in most hospitals in India. Soon, however, the baby is in his arms and he can adopt actions such as holding the baby, reading to, singing to, and cuddling his baby as a means of engrossment. In addition, he can help with baby chores like nappy changing, and taking over at bedtime. Dad needs to do some learning too just like Mom is doing and find ways to enjoy the moments of engrossment.

Bonding is important as it helps your baby thrive. It is essential for both parents to stay connected. Set aside time for yourselves to bond with your baby, and note that this bonding is going to last a lifetime.

Glossary

1. **Musculoskeletal system:** It is the system made up of bones, muscles and all the associated connective tissues that bind them together. This system provides form, support, stability and movement to the body (NIH Curriculum Supplement Series (Internet). Bethesda MD: the National Institutes of Health (US); 2007).

2. **Sepsis:** A severe form of infection.

3. **Sudden Infant Death Syndrome (SIDS):** The unexplained death of an infant who is less than a year old, that generally occurs while asleep. It is also known as cot death.

4. **Nursing nest:** A term used to describe a cozy, quiet spot where you can breastfeed your baby without being disturbed. You can set up a space such as this with a towel, glass of water to drink, and a pillow to elevate the baby to the proper position.

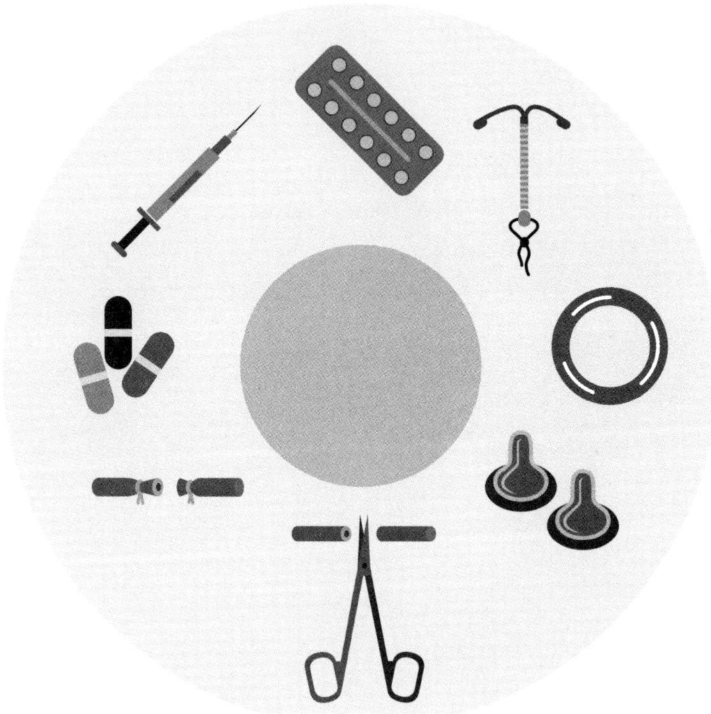

CHAPTER 13

Postnatal Guidance and Advice

DELIVERING A BABY is not the end of the chapter as a pregnant woman. Your postnatal concern is to recover physically and also to prevent another pregnancy in quick succession. It is best to consult your doctor to understand and navigate this phase.

Be aware that changes are taking place in your body during the six-week period of recuperation after delivery. The hormonal transformations that occurred during pregnancy revert to their pre-pregnancy levels and your biological clock is back to the pre-pregnancy mode. In other words, you are ready for pregnancy again!

At this time, it is imperative for you to learn about

contraception (preventing a pregnancy). Ask your doctor about the various methods available to you and seek his/her assistance in deciding on the approach most suitable for you. The options offered currently are Long Acting Reversible Contraceptives[1] (LARC), Progesterone Only Pills (POP) that are safe for breastfeeding, and various barrier methods. Seek your doctor's advice before you resume sexual activity as accidental pregnancies do happen.

You may have taken some precautionary vaccinations before pregnancy and others that may have been recommended and considered safe during pregnancy. The Federation of Obstetric and Gynaecological Societies of India (FOGSI) recommends being vaccinated against Rubella[2], Hepatitis B[3], Varicella or Chickenpox, Influenza, HPV[4], Tetanus[5], Whooping cough[6] and Diphtheria[7] now, in the postnatal phase, if they were not administered earlier. The HPV vaccine is an example of a vaccine that was not advisable during pregnancy but can now be taken. This is a vaccine that protects you from certain infections that can cause cancer of the cervix[8].

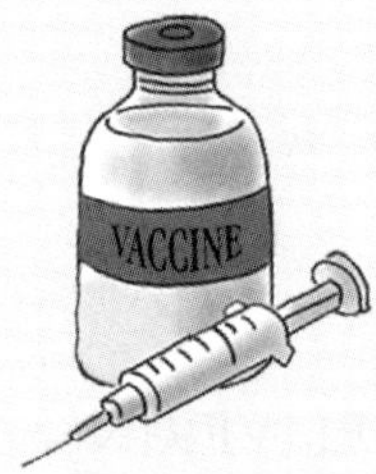

Figure 4

By this time you are longing to get back into your lovely, old but shapely clothes. To get ready, you can now discuss postnatal exercises with your doctor. You have probably resumed some warm-up exercises already, so chalk out a regular regimen with his or her advice.

Also, remember to enquire about a long-term program of follow-up visits regarding any medical conditions such as diabetes, high blood pressure or thyroid disorders that may have occurred while you were pregnant. Follow-up consultations may include blood tests and alteration of medication, if necessary. Your doctor may advise you to modify your lifestyle, with respect to dietary habits and exercise, in order to prevent full-fledged diabetes or high blood pressure in the future. As you may be aware, if left unchecked, these ailments can lead to heart problems including heart attacks.

If considering air travel with your infant, wait for at least two months after delivery, preferably more, to give the newborn a chance to build up his/her immunity. For the same reason, stay away from crowded places and postpone even brief outings prior to six weeks after delivery.

Spacing between pregnancies is desirable. Use contraceptives to prevent pregnancy too soon after delivery.

It is important to "space" pregnancies as it helps your newborn child grow with a feeling of security. A gap between two pregnancies can create an environment in which the new family can bond well. Before you plan to give your little one a playmate, recall the earlier advice in chapter 1 and head back to the doctor for pre-pregnancy counselling again.

Notes

FOGSI: The Federation of Obstetric and Gynaecological Societies of India is a professional organisation representing practitioners of obstetrics and gynaecology in India. According to their website it exists "to encourage and disseminate knowledge, education and research in the field of obstetrics and gynaecology."

Contraceptive methods launched by our Ministry of Health and Family Welfare

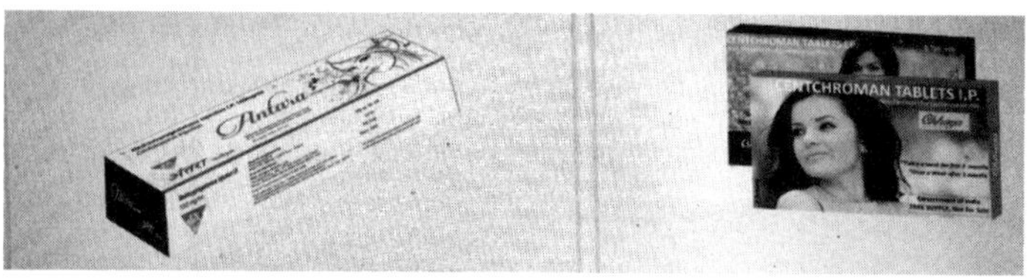

Anthara-3 monthly injection and chaaya-contraceptive pills

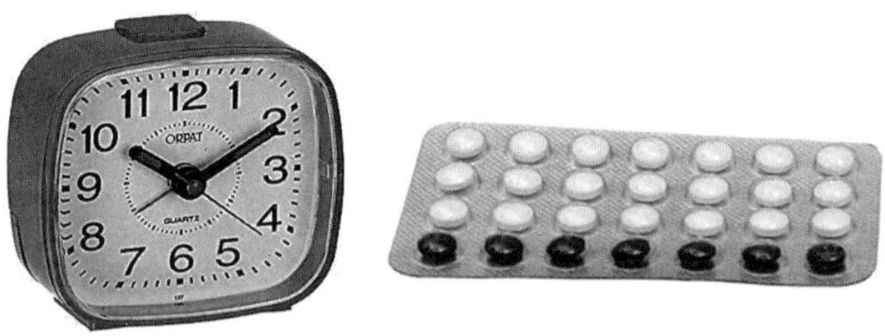

Birth control pills to be taken at the same time every night. Set an alarm as reminder!

Various contraceptive methods

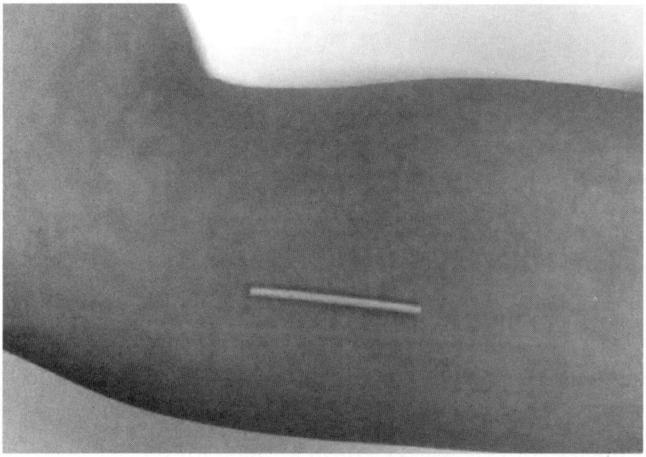

Injectable implants-Implanon

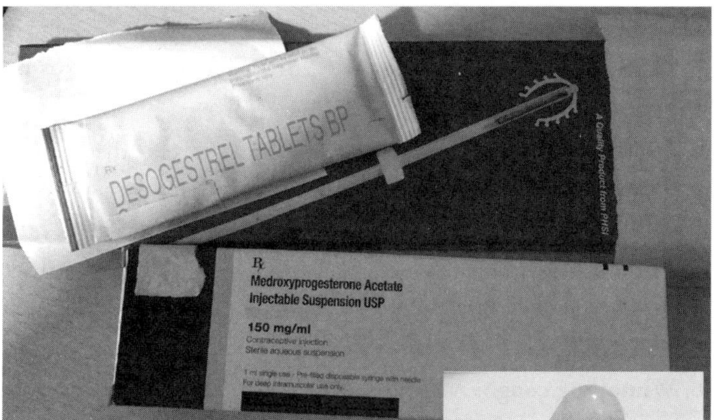

Pills and LARCS

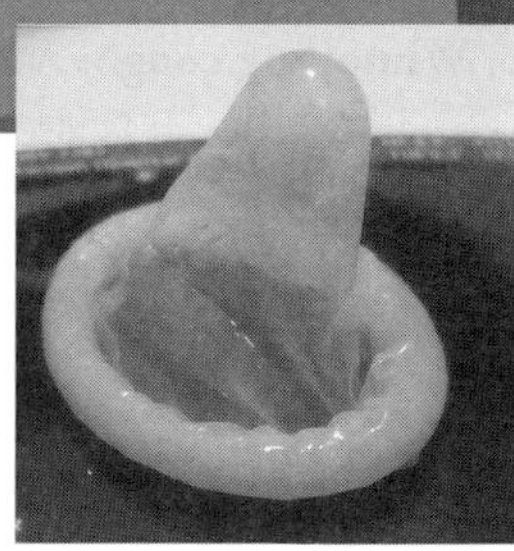

Barrier method

Glossary

1. **Long-Acting Reversible Contraceptives (LARCs):** They are a variety of hormonal and non-hormonal methods that are effective in preventing pregnancies for multiple years at a time without the need of any particular action by the user. They are reversible because the contraceptive action can be reversed to allow the woman to conceive if the couple wishes to have a baby.

2. **Rubella:** Also known as German Measles, Rubella is a viral infection that can create abnormalities in the foetus if acquired by the pregnant mother.

3. **Hepatitis B:** A viral infection of the liver due to the hepatitis B virus.

4. **HPV (Human Papillomavirus) vaccine:** A vaccine that prevents infection by certain types of HPV viruses. These sexually transmitted viruses can cause genital warts and cervical cancer.

5. **Tetanus:** Also known as lockjaw, tetanus is a serious bacterial infection that affects the nerves controlling muscle movement, resulting in severe muscle spasms.

6. **Whooping cough:** A highly contagious bacterial infection of the nose and throat. It is also known as pertussis.

7. **Diphtheria:** An infectious, contagious disease which primarily affects the nose and throat.

8. **Cervix:** Narrow neck like passage forming the lower end of the uterus or womb.

Frequently Asked Questions (FAQs)

I'm a veterinary surgeon with a thyroid problem. Do I need to stop my thyroid medication now as I am planning to conceive?

This is a classic situation where the role of pre-pregnancy counselling is demonstrably important.
It is vital to consult your doctor before stopping any medication on your own. Besides, in your case, it is crucial to inform your doctor that you are a veterinary surgeon as you are regularly exposed to infections arising from proximity to animals. For example, you will need protection against an infection like toxoplasmosis[1] from cats. If you get pregnant while you are infected it can be harmful to your baby via Mother to Child Transmission (MTCT).

What do I have to do to have a normal delivery?

I agree that most women would like to have a normal or vaginal delivery. There is nothing you can do specifically to have a normal delivery but it certainly helps to be active and go about your usual routine. Be sure to include a 30-minute walk and if you attend an antenatal class then do the exercises you may have learnt there. Any effort, such as this, will keep your muscles supple and strong so you can cope well with any kind of delivery. Further, if your pregnancy has no risk factors the probability of having a normal delivery is high.

I am not gaining enough weight. Is it a cause for concern?

The total weight gained in pregnancy is 10 to 12 kg, most of which occurs when the foetus begins to grow after 20 weeks of pregnancy. It is possible that the foetus is fine and well, although you are not gaining weight. The doctor will determine whether the foetus is indeed growing, sometimes using an ultrasound test. If, however, foetal growth is not advancing as expected, then the doctor will judge whether inadequate nutrition or something else, such as high blood pressure is restricting growth indirectly.

Are all the Over-the-counter (OTC) drugs safe in pregnancy?

No, some are not. So, it is safer to take the medicines prescribed to you by your doctor. Even common painkillers with ibuprofen and nimesulide, for example, are not safe during pregnancy, particularly if consumed after the sixth month. These medications can reduce the amniotic fluid and also create a heart problem in the foetus. The application of ointments to reduce pain is also discouraged.

Is it safe to get ultrasound tests done in pregnancy?

Ultrasound scanning is considered safe as the technology is based on sound waves. There is no exposure to radiation as in the case of X-rays.

I am an anaesthesiologist. Should I be concerned about the effects of "inhaler gases"[2] that I might be exposed to?

Studies have found that while there is no evidence to suggest any link between "inhaler gases" and abnormalities in the foetus, there is a slightly higher risk of having an abortion as compared to the general population if you are exposed to them.

Is it true that my baby's Intelligence Quotient (IQ) will be high if I consume Docosahexaenoic Acid[3] (DHA) during pregnancy?

It is believed that DHA is beneficial during pregnancy and also for the baby after birth, although there is no evidence supporting this claim.

What is "painless labour"?

There are various ways in medical practice to help a woman go through labour in a relatively smooth way, in spite of experiencing severe pains. Sometimes one's husband or a close attendant is allowed to be present to support you throughout the process until you are taken into the delivery room. A gentle massage to your back and thighs can give you immense relief, both physically and psychologically. Certain drugs are designed to help you bear the pain even though they do not necessarily provide complete relief. Pain relieving drugs[4] are administered by injecting either into a muscle or into a space in the spinal cord (see Epidural analgesia[5] in the glossary). Listening to soothing music also alleviates pain to a significant extent because it is relaxing.

Is it true that consuming papaya in pregnancy can cause an abortion?

Unripe papaya is known to be rich in latex[6] which can stimulate uterine contractions, so it is best to cook it before consumption.

Is it problematic to wear high-heeled footwear in pregnancy?

High-heeled footwear can strain the back. Ideally, you should wear soft-soled footwear with a 1" heel. Absolutely flat footwear is also not recommended.

Why do I feel too lethargic to even take a walk?

You probably find that you are unable to walk beyond 10 to 15 minutes at a stretch because you get tired and suffer from backache. But this is not a reason to be sedentary. If you cannot walk for 30 to 40 minutes continuously then try, instead, to walk for 15 minutes at a time upto three times daily. The feeling of lethargy should gradually disappear as you increase your activity. If you still continue to feel tired then consult the doctor.

Is it normal to keep feeling pain above my navel but more accurately to the sides and below the rib/bony area?

As pregnancy advances the growing womb occupies the space where the intestines normally rest. It is not surprising to feel pain in the area described. The loops of the intestines get displaced upwards to the area below the rib cage, which can result in pain. Also, you may experience pain due to gaseous distension in the intestines. Eat small meals frequently, to avoid bloating. Further, as intestinal movement is slow during pregnancy there may be some delay in finally feeling relieved. Walking can help to make you feel better. Another way to cope is to assume an inclined position when sitting as it creates more space between the ribs and the womb.

How frequently should my baby kick?

You should feel your baby's kicks all the time from the fifth month onwards. The maximum number of kicks are felt around the 30th to 32nd week of pregnancy. Subsequently the number of movements reduce due to the increase in size of the baby. But as you approach the due date, around 37 weeks, at least 1-2 movements should be felt within an hour. Be aware that there may be simple explanations for why, sometimes, you are not actually perceiving movements within an hour. A baby sleeps for about 40 minutes at a stretch, several times a day. So, it is possible for you to miss the gap between two stretches and not notice any movements within an hour. Your baby could be hungry or you may be suffering from a lot of gaseous distension and consequently, finding it difficult to discern movements. Have some juice and an antacid to relieve the bloating and if you still do not feel your baby moving subsequently, then you should report to the hospital. At other times, the baby may be in an awkward position in the uterus. The baby's back may have flipped towards your front or the position of the placenta[7] is in front of the uterus. This is also a kind of situation when you may not feel the baby moving well.

Recall from chapter 10 that the placenta is a flattened circular organ filled with blood vessels. It is attached to the uterus on one side and provides nutrients and oxygen to the baby through the umbilical cord which is attached to its inner surface.

LABOUR AND DELIVERY

What if my water bag breaks before labour pains begin?

This can happen in a small percentage of women, but labour pains should normally start spontaneously a few hours later. You should report to the hospital where the doctor will give you medicine to induce pains, if they haven't already begun.

I want to go to my hometown for delivery. What is the latest period to travel?

If travelling by train the latest period would be when you are 36 weeks into the pregnancy. Beyond this period, although uncommon, the swaying movement of the train has been known to stimulate uterine contractions in pregnant women. Avoid long distance travel by road, whether it is by car or bus, as sitting continuously and passing over treacherous roads can be risky. As far as airlines are concerned, each airline has its own rules limiting travel by expectant mothers based on the number of weeks of pregnancy the woman has completed. It is wise for you to consult your future obstetrician at least by 36 weeks. This way you and your doctor can get acquainted with each other and the doctor has a chance to learn the details about your pregnancy.

CAESAREAN SECTION (C-SECTION)

The doctor told me everything was normal yet when I got into labour, why did I need a C-section?

Assuming you consented to the C-section procedure, the doctor must have explained the circumstances that led to it becoming necessary, in your specific case. Even if you had no risk factors, some conditions show up during labour which warrant an immediate caesarean operation. A fall in the heart rate of the baby or a rise above the range (110-160 beats /minute), over a long period, is considered an emergency. The baby's heart rate is monitored using a method called cardiotocography[8] (CTG) in which traces of the heart beats are recorded on a graph strip. A fall or rise in the heart rate as indicated by the trace implies that the foetus may be in some kind of trouble. If the colour and consistency of the amniotic fluid appear green and thick when the water bag bursts in active labour, then it is an emergency as it indicates that the foetus is in distress. In some cases, the foetal head is unable to enter the bony passage or even if it does it faces the risk of getting jammed because the passage is not wide enough. These are some possible problematic situations when a doctor may consider a C-section necessary.

I choose to have a C-section and my husband supports me in this decision. I do not want to suffer through severe labour pains. Also, the possibility that a lax vagina after vaginal delivery can cause a lack of sexual interest, prompts me to prefer a C-section to a vaginal delivery. Is it okay to opt for it?

There are many factors to consider with respect to the options before you. Firstly, the doctor will counsel you about available effective ways to cope with labour pains and also tell you about the pros and cons of opting to go through a C-section. With a vaginal delivery your hospital stay may be shorter than in the case of a C-section which is, after all, a surgery. On the other hand, as you already know, a lax vagina and prolapse of the uterus (sliding out of the uterus) in old age is a possibility after a vaginal delivery. In addition, you may experience incontinence of urine temporarily. With the surgical option, since the probability of complications increases with each additional C-section, the overall effect is that it limits the total number of children you can expect to have. Also, being a surgery, there can be complications from anaesthesia and excessive bleeding.

Babies delivered by C-section before 39 weeks may need to be monitored in a nursery, due to respiratory problems.

When you opt for a C-section you will have to sign a separate form to consent to a "Caesarean Delivery on Maternal Request" or CDMR. The doctor may suggest that you consult another gynaecologist also before confirming your decision.

My previous delivery was by a C-section. I am 9 months pregnant. What are the chances of having a normal delivery now?

This is not uncommon as almost 70% of women deliver normally after a C-section. However, there are certain criteria to be met. The doctor will discuss them with you in detail, based on records of your previous delivery. A vaginal birth after C-section (VBAC) can be attempted once you provide an informed consent, following the discussion.

My last ultrasound showed that there is a loop of cord around the baby's neck. Does that mean that I will have a C-section?

Having the cord looping around the baby's neck is usually not a reason, by itself, for a caesarean delivery. Pay attention to foetal movements and if you perceive a decrease then you should report to the hospital. If already in labour, the doctor will monitor the foetal heart rate and resort to surgery if there is a fall in the rate.

Why is it an emergency if my baby does "POTTY"?

POTTY turns the normally clear amniotic fluid green. Typically, the baby passes stools, called meconium soon after delivery. However, if this happens before delivery or during labour, then it can mean that the baby is in some distress. He or she may be in some kind of trouble due to which the anal opening suddenly opens up and the baby is unable to prevent the stools from exiting the body. If the fluid is thick and greenish it can be swallowed by the baby and even enter the lungs creating a problem called Meconium Aspiration Syndrome. In this instance, the baby may require ventilation to assist in breathing.

I delivered last night but I do not seem to have adequate breast milk. Why?

There is no cause for concern at this stage. Secretion of milk is initiated by early skin to skin contact and suckling of the breast. (The mother to baby skin to skin contact is termed Kangaroo Care[9]). Subsequently, the secretion increases with frequent suckling. The first few feeds of the baby consist of Colostrum, a thick yellowish milk that is rich in proteins and antibodies, which protects the baby against chest and stomach infections. Breast milk is established by the 4th or 5th day.

I delivered my baby girl two days ago. I was stunned to see her have a slight blood stained discharge from the vagina. Is this normal?

There is nothing to be alarmed about a blood stained discharge from your infant as it will subside on its own.

It is notably seen in girl babies. Hormones from your bloodstream reach the baby through the placenta. Once born, girl babies tend to have the discharge due to withdrawal of the hormones from you.

Is it okay to use diapers on my baby? I am particularly concerned about diaper rash.

As such, it is preferable to use washable cloth diapers rather than those constructed with plastic. Change them frequently. Air out the baby's bottom once in a while. Many creams with zinc oxide as a common ingredient are available commercially to prevent and heal diaper rash. But some home remedies are also quite effective. You can apply vaseline, virgin coconut oil or olive oil. Alternatively, believe it or not, you can clean the affected red area using breast milk!

I have 2 children and both were delivered by caesarean sections. My younger child is 3 years old and we are not keen on having anymore children. What can we do to prevent future pregnancies?

If you feel absolutely sure that you have completed your family then the sterilisation[10] procedure is a good option. As you have already had 2 surgeries it would be better if your husband underwent a procedure called Vasectomy[11]. Besides being simpler than the sterilisation procedure in women, vasectomy also has higher success rates. It is a myth that there is loss of libido (sexual drive) after vasectomy. You also have the option of getting an Intrauterine Device[12] (IUD) inserted.

How soon can I start exercising after a C-section?

In principle, as any wound takes 6 weeks to heal, it is best to avoid doing strenuous exercises until after this period. You can build up your exercise regimen gradually. If you feel up to it, you can start with simple pelvic floor exercises a week after discharge from the hospital. Introduce low impact exercises like walking and light yoga 6 weeks later. Swimming is an option provided there is no bleeding. You can begin core abdominal exercises about 3 to 4 months after delivery.

I had a Thyroid problem and high sugars only during pregnancy. Do I need to continue the thyroid medication and rigorous diet to keep my blood sugars under check?

It is very important for you to consult your doctor after delivery, who will then repeat the thyroid and blood sugar tests 6 weeks later and advise you based on the results. If you were avoiding unnecessary sweets during pregnancy, why not continue the habit as this will help you in the long run anyway!

I will be going to my mother's place for 3 months. When can I adopt a family planning measure?

Your body is ready for another pregnancy 6 weeks after delivery, so your husband should at least follow the barrier method (condoms) of contraception if he visits you while you are there. Or you can get the Copper T[13] method of contraception done or take the first dose of the 3 monthly hormone injections during your visit.

Is it true that consuming milk after the operation will cause infection of my caesarean wound?

Absolutely not true.

My folks at home insist I restrict my water intake after delivery as it will give me a big tummy later on. Is it right?

Not according to modern science. In fact, there is a real danger of reporting back to the hospital after contracting severe urinary problems and high fever, as a result of dehydration caused by not drinking enough liquid. As long as you drink 2 to 2.5 litres of any kind of fluid per day, including water, you should be fine.

When can I resume sexual activity after delivery?

Whether childbirth is due to vaginal delivery or a C-section, it takes 6 weeks to heal as with any wound. So you can resume sexual activity preferably after this period. Remember, however, that your body is simultaneously ready for another pregnancy. Consult the doctor about contraception before resuming sexual activity in order to prevent an accidental pregnancy or to learn about spacing pregnancy, if interested in another child again.

My mother wants to know when I can start eating homemade preparations like dry fruits with ghee and jaggery after my delivery. When can I expect to do so?

There is no hard and fast rule but consuming rich food soon after delivery may cause discomfort in the tummy.

You can consume them when your body has recovered a little, generally 1 week after a normal delivery and 2 weeks after a C-section.

Is it true that except for the barrier approach (condoms) to contraception, I will gain weight using all other forms of contraception, as they are hormonal?

This idea is a misconception as it is not true. The intrauterine device (IUD) that is most commonly used is not hormonal although hormonal varieties are also available. The non-hormonal type of IUD does not cause an increase in weight. Tablets and injections are hormonal but the weight you gain from them is minimal and even then, only when used over a long period of time.

My husband and I are not keen on having more than one child. Can I go through a permanent method of birth control?

Sterilisation or tubal ligation is a permanent method for birth control. It is advisable that this method, which has its pros and cons, is best followed when your existing child is at least 5 years old. Even at that point you can opt for a Long-acting Reversible Contraceptive[14] (LARC method as mentioned in chapter 13 and in the glossary). In my practice, I have seen several women regret their decision, years later. You should be absolutely sure before going in for permanent birth control.

Glossary

1. **Toxoplasmosis:** A parasitic infection (one due to an organism living in the body as a parasite) that can threaten the health of an unborn child.

2. **Inhaler gases:** The context in question 6 above refers to an anaesthetic gas. It is delivered by getting the patient to inhale it by using a face mask prior to anaesthetizing the patient.

3. **Docosahexaenoic Acid (DHA):** An omega-3 fatty acid necessary for growth and functional development of the brain.

4. Pain relieving drugs: Medications used to provide relief from pain. Tramadol is an example of pain relieving drugs belonging to a group known as Opioids.

5. **Epidural analgesia:** A way in which pain relieving medication is injected into a space called the "epidural space" in the spinal cord. This method is used to provide relief to a woman in labour during childbirth.

6. **Latex (in papaya):** The milky fluid that oozes when some plants or their fruits are cut or scored (creating fine grooves on the surface with the tip of a knife) is called latex. When the neck of a raw papaya is scored latex exudes from it and is collected for various beneficial purposes. However, its consumption by pregnant women is discouraged because latex is known to cause contractions of the uterus.

7. **Placenta:** A flattened circular organ that is filled with blood vessels. It is attached to the uterus on one side and provides nutrients and oxygen to the baby through the umbilical cord, which is attached to its inner surface.

8. **Cardiotocography (CTG):** A CTG is a technological way to record fetal heart sounds on a graph while the mother simultaneously intimates foetal movements by pressing a button. The method is used to monitor foetal well-being. The doctor interprets the graph to determine if a C-section is needed.

9. **Kangaroo care:** Skin to skin /chest to chest contact of mother with her baby who has only a diaper on. This helps in bonding, better temperature control, higher likelihood of successful breastfeeding, especially in preterm babies.

10. **Sterilisation:** A procedure to prevent fertilisation by tying/ cutting of the tubes through which sperm travels, in order to prevent pregnancy.

11. **Vasectomy:** A birth control method that the husband undergoes in which the tubes that transport sperm, called the vas deferens, are cut and tied.

12. **Intrauterine Device (IUD):** Small T-shaped plastic contraceptive device placed inside the uterus to block sperm from reaching an egg and thus preventing fertilisation. Both hormonal and non-hormonal varieties exist.

13. **Copper T:** This is a kind of non-hormonal intrauterine device or IUD which is a T-shaped flexible piece of plastic, with a copper wire wound around it, that is inserted into the uterus to prevent pregnancy. The copper in the IUD destroys the sperms when they enter the uterus.

14. **Long-Acting Reversible Contraceptives (LARCs):** They are a variety of hormonal and non-hormonal methods that are effective in preventing pregnancies for multiple years at a time without the need of any particular action by the user. They are reversible because the contraceptive action can be reversed to allow the woman to conceive if the couple wishes to have a baby.

References

Unveiling the Mysteries Within

1. Julie A Mannella, PhD, Coren P Jagnow, MS, and Gary K Beauchamp, PhD (2001): "Prenatal and Postnatal Flavor Learning by Human Infants". Pediatrics 107 (6), e88-e88, 2001.

2. Sumit Jha (2007): Comments by Girija Devi in "Ragas to Riches for Kids", *Times of India*; April 6, 2007.

3. Eino Partanen, Teija Kujala, and Minna Huotilainen (2013): "Prenatal Music Exposure Induces Long-Term Neural Effects", PLoS One. 2013; v.8(10); e78946. Published online 2013, October 30, doi: 10.1371/journal.pone.0078946.

4. Kanenishi K, Hanaoka U, Noguchi J, Marumo G, and Hata T (2013): "4D Ultrasound Evaluation of Fetal Facial Expressions During the Latter Stages of the Second Trimester", Int. J Gynaecol Obstet 2013 June; 121(3):257-60. doi:10.1016/j.ijgo.2013.01.018. Epub 2013 March 14.

A Pregnancy Spread—Nurturing with Nutrition

1. American College of Obstetricians and Gynecologists (ACOG) 2010: "Moderate Caffeine Consumption During Pregnancy", American College of Obstetricians and Gynecologists, No 462, August 2010. Reaffirmed 2016.

Challenges to a Beautiful Pregnancy

1. American College of Obstetricians and Gynecologists (ACOG): Book: "*Your Pregnancy and Childbirth – Month to Month,*" Revised Sixth Edition, 2015.

Mild to Moderate Workouts, not Burnouts

1. British Wheel of Yoga: According to their website, this is "the largest yoga membership organization in the UK, committed to promoting a greater understanding of yoga and its safe practice through experience, education, study and training." www.bwy.org.uk